2019 Edition

YOU'RE PLANNING A B'NAI MITZVAH

A **D**o-**I**t-**Y**ourself-**W**ith-**H**elp guide for planning, organizing, and creating your special simcha!

B'nai Mitzvah Planning Made Easy
Cara Weiss and SAVE *The* DATE, LLC EVENTS
OVER 25 years of professional & certified planning experience all in one guide

---

© **SAVE *The* DATE, LLC EVENTS**
events and promotions your way
WWW.SaveTheDateLLCEvents.com

AWARD WINNING, EVENT PLANNING, AND EDUCATING FOR OVER 25 YEARS

@SAVETHEDATELLCEVENTS
TWITTER: @SAVETHEDATELLC
FEAUTURED SPEAKER AT THE SPECIAL EVENT,
EVENT SOLUTIONS, & CATERSOURCE
FEATURED PROFESSOR AT MONTGOMERY COLLEGE
CONTINUING EDUCATION 2019, 2020

© SAVE *The* DATE, LLC EVENTS
events and promotions your way
WWW.SaveTheDateLLCEvents.com

TABLE OF CONTENTS

Section 1: So You're Planning a Mitzvah Party! 7
    Organizing Calendar 10
    Questions to Get You Started 14
    The Day of your Event 16
    Compromising 17
    Vendor Obligations 18
    Client Profile Sheet 19

Section 2: Calculating the Costs 21
    Negotiating 22
    Average Prices 23
    Sample Budget 1 24
    Sample Budget 2 25
    Sample Budget 3 26
    Sample Budget 4 27
    Vendor Tipping 28
    Your Budget 29

Section 3: Event Planner 31
    Party Planner Info Sheet 32
    "Day of" Director 33
    Day-of Director Info Sheet 35

Section 4: Temple and Religion 37
    Temple Information Sheet 39
    Temple Décor 40
    Temple Oneg Information Sheet 41
    Aliyah 42
    Mitzvah Project 43
    Candle Lighting Ceremony 44
    Shabbat Dinner 45
    Shabbat Dinner Information Sheet 46

Section 5: Your Venue 47
    Questions to Ask and Things to Consider 48
    Questions to Ask at Initial Site Inspection 51
    Considering the Outdoors 54

Request for Proposal (RFP) 55

Venue Information Sheet 56

Section 6: Catering 57

Contract 58

Catering Information Sheet 59

Cake 60

Celebrate with Food, Dancing and Drink 61

Bar 62

Section 7: Entertainment 63

Your Music Selections 64

Band/MC/DJ Information Sheet 65

Fun and Games 66

Actors as Entertainment 67

Actor(s) Information Sheet 68

Section 8: Photography/Videography 69

Photography Information Sheet 72

Videography 73

Videography Information Sheet 74

Montage 75

Creating and Organizing Your Montage 76

Montage Information Sheet 78

Section 9: Décor 79

Décor consists of the following items 80

Flowers and Décor Information Sheet 81

Themes 82

Balloons/Decorations Information Sheet 83

Lighting 84

Lighting Information Sheet 85

Section 10: Rentals and Favors 86

Rentals Information Sheet 87

Linen Rentals Information Sheet 88

Parking/Transportation 89

Valet Information Sheet 90

Transportation Information Sheet 91

Security 92

Security Information Sheet 93

SECTION 11: Favors and Branding 94
Favors Information Sheet 95

Branding your party with a logo 96

Other Items 98

Other Retail Information Sheet 99

Section 12: Invitations 101
Invitation Information Sheet 103

Items Needed for Invitations 104

Sample Invitation 105

Sample Invitation Phrases 106

Sample Invitation Response Cards 108

Hebrew Phrases 109

Now Draft Your Own Invitation! 110

Section 13: Other Printing 111
Other Printing Information Sheet 112

Out of Town Guest Letter 113

Welcome Basket Information Sheet 114

Sample Welcome Letter 115

Sample Friends and Family Letter 116

Sample Parent/Children Letter 118

The Program 120

Sample Program 121

Place Cards 124

Section 14: Scheduling 125
Mitzvah Long Schedule 126

Mitzvah Short Schedule 128

Day of the Event 136

Items To Deliver Or To Bring Along 137

Mitzvah Event Checklist 139

Section 15: Guests 143

Attire Information Sheet 144

Your Guests 145

Seating 146

Layout 147

Layout Samples 148

Section 16: After the Event 152

Next-Day Brunch Information Sheet 154

Miscellaneous Expenses Information Sheet 155

SECTION 1: SO YOU'RE PLANNING A MITZVAH PARTY!

So, you have a date! The mitzvah is an important step in any child's life and even though your date may be several years away, planning now will make your event better–so use the following pages as a guide to begin thinking about and planning for your party.

Keep in mind:
- Remember what this day symbolizes in relationship to your God, temple and family members.
- This is your party—there are no rules, so what you and your family wants is primary.
- Organization is essential; if you are organized, the planning process and the actual party will run smoothly. Our staff at SAVE *The* DATE are knowledgeable professionals with decades of experience, so if you are looking at this huge project with butterflies in your stomach, we can help! Keep your whole family, especially the honoree, involved in the planning process.
- Don't forget your budget.
- On the day of your party, you may want to have someone monitor the party and see to your needs especially the "day of" so you may enjoy your own party! Ask SAVE *The* DATE for more information about the "day-of" services.

Good luck!

Understanding The B'nai Mitzvah

What is the B'nai Mitzvah?
- Taking a step into adulthood by reading from the Torah and performing your Bar/Bat Mitzvah duties.
- Understanding the type of person you want to be

Who is a Bar/Bat Mitzvah?
- Jewish children or adults who have not yet had the privilege of reading from the Torah
- Must be 13 year old or older (some temples allow girls to be 12 because it is recognized that girls mature earlier)

What is a Bar/Bat Mitzvah?
- An honor, privilege, and a tradition
- The privilege of reading/chanting directly out of the Torah in front of family, friends, and peers
- The recognition that you have studied your faith and have a basic understanding of your role in the world.

Why are you doing all of this?
Your child will learn a Torah portion then run services and lead many prayers. The Torah is written in Hebrew as a form of rules/laws for the Jewish people to live by. Sung using a system called trope, symbols represent musical symbols that are soon recognized and easily sung in a similar tune.

Some temples require your child to learn and lead a Haftorah, a minimized version of the Torah, as well. There are many theories of what Haftorah truly is. One is The Haftorah was written at a time when The Samaritans did not allow Jews to "read" Torah. This version of the Torah was written in book form to allow Jews to study without the Samaritan's knowledge.

Your child will sing their Torah portion out of the actual Torah and the Haftorah will probably be out of a book or sheet given to your child.

Your child will write and recite in his own words a lesson to teach the congregation how to interpret and understand their Torah portion. There is no limit on the interpretations.

Your child may be asked to read, interpret, write a speech about, and quote from a book of "good deeds" called The Divar Torah/Pirkei Avot.

Some temples practice Pirkei Avot, which is a book of historical readings that include passages of rabbinical moral and ethical teachings that Jewish people try to live by. This, they believe, distinguishes them as a moral Jewish person. Some temples have your child study and read from the Haftorah to sing and explain, in their own words, a grown-up story or concept from the Torah and assist in leading the service. Learning Torah Trope show friends and family that the new adult has found his/her place in the world, so invite people to see your accomplishments. Sometimes, this privilege is shared with another temple member, but the celebrations are typically separate. A celebration of food, dancing, and drink follows, in fact, Jewish custom follows all celebrations with food and drink.

Organizing Calendar

Immediately, as soon as you decide your date …
- find a planner
- begin researching venues
- contact your "partner Mitzvah" to say hello
- put the date on all family calendars
- decide on the type of Simcha
- begin a guest list to get an estimate
- open a separate bank account and set an affordable budget

2 Years Before
- begin researching bands, DJ's and Master of Ceremonies (MC)
- have your child begin learning their Torah portion
- begin researching caterers
- think about themes
- create a schedule (see long schedule)

1 ½ Years Before
- have your music booked
- begin discussing themes and colors with your child
- begin looking at save-the-date cards
- begin researching photographers and videographers
- contract with a hotel for a room block and rate
- contract with a caterer
- update schedule

1 Year Before
- book your photographer and videographer
- decide on the theme and colors
- begin to research decorators/florists
- order personal tallit and kippot
- update schedule
- begin to design a layout (see layout sample)

9 Months Before
start shopping for attire—girls cover their shoulders at Temple and everyone may want another dress for the evening celebration

© SAVE The DATE, LLC EVENTS
events and promotions your way
WWW.SaveTheDateLLCEvents.com

- draft the invitation wording
- book transportation and valet
- begin writing down ideas for the logo/slogan
- update schedule

8 Months Before
- choose imprinted kippot for guests and fill out forms
- begin contracting with a décor company
- begin looking into "other entertainment" options
- begin thinking about "out of towners"
- begin thinking about Shabbat dinner
- begin getting lighting proposals
- make list of table names
- if you want a cake, contract a cake vendor
- have the venue provide a blank layout with dimensions
- meet with rental companies for any rentals
- update schedule

7 Months Before
- begin looking at invitation designs
- finalize guest list: type all names and addresses in Microsoft Excel so they can be sorted later by first name for name tags, rsvp for a count, or columns of who sits where.
- begin to consider mitzvah projects
- begin candle lighting speech
- send 'Save The Dates,' by mail or electronically
- update schedule

6 Months Before
- make final selections for mitzvah dresses
- create a contract with other entertainment vendor(s)
- decide on party favors
- order tchotchkes as giveaways (DJ may provide)
- begin trope lessons
- begin writing a friends and family letter
- place order for invitation and proof

update schedule

5 Months Before
- approve your invitation and weight it for postage
- order stamps for invitations and RSVP cards
- schedule a calligrapher to address envelopes
- schedule hair, make-up, and nail appointments
- update schedule

4 Months Before
- purchase all items named above
- make song list for musician(s)
- make photo list for photographer
- write the children's letter
- discuss arrangements for kippot/kiddush with partner mitzvah family
- begin shopping for other items needed for mitzvah
- begin writing speeches
- begin thinking about mitzvah favors
- begin looking for men's and boy's suits
- update schedule

3 Months Before
- assemble invitations and mail
- mail the friends and family letter
- begin organizing hotel welcome baskets
- buy gifts for rabbi, tutor and cantor
- purchase prizes for games
- finalize décor
- order thank you cards
- finalize contracts for brunch and Shabbat dinner
- decide on place cards
- make arrangements for the family pet(s)
- update schedule

2 Months Before
- go to tasting and finalize catering menu
- begin seating arrangements and assignments
- finalize children's letter
- book security

update schedule

1 Month Before
- write final checks to vendors
- finalize seating arrangements and assignments
- finish script for candle lighting
- finish speeches
- finish mitzvah arrangements
- test video montage on equipment
- update schedule
- update layout

1 Week Before
- prepare final checks for day of and vendor tips
- confirm arrangements with all vendors
- prepare all papers for planner and caterer
- finish place cards
- prepare a short schedule (see short schedule)
- finalize schedule, email long and short schedule, layout and logo to all vendors

3 Days Before
- deliver hotel welcome baskets
- deliver Box A ceremony and Box B reception items
- give caterer final guarantee
- wash cars
- finish paying the planner's contract and confirm all times
- take formal photos at bima

The Day of the Party
- relax and have fun!

After the Party
- write thank you letters
- review photos, order photo albums; expect your final album and video within 6 months (after you pick and approve photos/video footage)
- continue with confirmation
- continue doing mitzvahs

Questions to Get You Started

Who are your favorite artists? bands? musicians?

Where is your favorite restaurant? vacation spot?

What is your favorite activity?
… book?
… car?
… color/s?
… clothing line?
… flower?
… food?
… game?
… hobby?
… movie?
… song?
… sport/team?
… TV show?

Do you prefer the city or the country?

Do you like animals? What is your favorite animal?

What is your dream?

What makes you happy?

What makes you special?

Now imagine your "dream event":
- Where would you like your event to take place?
- How many guests would attend?
- Will there be more kids or adults?
- Would there be a particular theme?
- What kind of atmosphere would there be (formal, informal, somewhere in-between)?

- Will you have a cocktail hour?
- What would the menu be and how would food be served (hors d'oeuvres, buffet-style, a sit-down meal, etc.)?
- Will you have different menu choices for kids and adults?
- What will the décor be for tables, chairs, linens, centerpieces, balloons, lighting?
- Will there be "special" décor items like ice sculptures or a backdrop?
- Will you include a candle lighting ceremony?
- Will you include a challah?
- What kind of entertainment and/or activities would you want (a DJ, a band, dancing, a magician, casino games, etc.)?
- What kind of favors would you give to your guests?
- Will you need to hire any security guards? (young guests should never be allowed to leave the party or party area without a parent)
- What is your budget and how does it all fit together?

The Day of your Event

You may want to ask certain people to do particular jobs or tasks before, during, and after your event.

During:
- designated "go-for" to help you/your family
- provide you and/or the honoree with an "escape route" (for example in case you get stuck talking to someone and can't get away)
- occupy younger children
- monitor the music, entertainment, catering and bar service
- offer vendors and offer food, drinks, or logistics
- direct photographer and videographer to ensure equipment is working properly and important moments are being photographed/filmed (speeches, the candle lighting ceremony, etc.)
- take photographs with a personal camera so nothing is missed
- film video with a personal video camera, to add to the inventory and angles
- monitor valet services and parking

Before and after:
- collect and hold checks and envelopes
- monitor the reception venue during and after the ceremony to make sure things go as planned (setting up, decorating, lost and found, etc.)
- bring important items to the ceremony and/or the reception - cameras, kippots, candles, a challah knife, etc.
- collect important ceremony items like programs
- collect important reception items at the end of the event (centerpieces, cameras, extra favors, etc.
- assist in packing your car at the end of the event
- collect and deliver gifts

> **NOTE:** Ask for more information about **SAVE** *The* **DATE** "day-of" services that takes care of all of the above and so much more.

Compromising

Disagreements arise in any family while planning food, music, decorations, and such a complicated event. Everyone wants the same outcome—a successful day and launching a boy or girl into adulthood with dignity and fun! To keep everyone happy, try to compromise. Ask everyone involved in the planning process to fill out the following on deadline, and then see what can be worked into the overall plan:

Very important ideas or must haves:

Idea:

Reason:

Idea:

Reason:

Idea:

Reason:

Idea:

Reason:

Vendor Obligations

A vendor is anyone hired or paid to work with you on your event. Vendors should be treated as you would treat a worker you trust to invite into in your home. You are not obligated to "take care" of them, however, remember basic human decency. Your vendors are working for you starting at least an hour before your event starts to at least an hour after your event ends, often 7 or 8 hours.

- They need to eat, drink, and take breaks to stay focused.
- Consider your vendors working on-site and preorder some basic meals for them to eat at an appropriate time in a back room.
- This lets them know not to eat your guest's food because you are providing for them. Your caterer should help you provide these meals for a nominal fee.
- Keep vendors on the same page by sending copies of schedules and contact information to everyone working for you at your celebration.
- Vendors are more efficient when their clients are organized. Send a Client Profile Sheet to all your vendors.

Tipping is optional but in general, anyone you know personally or who you feel went above and beyond the call of duty.
- Band, DJ, MC and team
- Banquet Captain
- Catering manager
- Party Planner
- Rabbi and cantor (discretionary fund contribution).

Client Profile Sheet

Client

Name:

Office:

Email:

Cell:

Fax:

Address:

Co-Client name:
Office:
Cell:
Fax:
Email:
Address:

Planner

Name:

Office:

Email:

Cell:

Fax:

Address:

Event

Type of event:

Date:

Time:

Approximate number of Guests (kids vs adults):

Theme of party:

Guest of honor:

Brothers/sisters names and ages:

Location of service:

Location of party:

Notes:

Photo of Client:

© SAVE *The* DATE, LLC EVENTS

events and promotions your way
WWW.SaveTheDateLLCEvents.com

SECTION 2: CALCULATING THE COSTS

Make sure your budget includes any potential costs for the following:

- attire and beauty services
- band, DJ, or MC package (screens, stage/platform, dancers, lighting)
- bars, liquor, sommelier, bartenders
- cake(s)
- catering and food service costs
- ceremony costs for the service at the temple
- dinner the evening before
- entertainment
- favors or gift bags
- flowers and décor
- going away breakfast/brunch the following day
- invitations (including calligraphy and postage)
- kippot
- lighting
- montage
- photographer
- planner
- planner for "day of"
- prizes for games
- program (writing, editing, printing)
- rabbi and tutor
- rental items (including tables, chairs, linens, etc.)
- tips
- transportation from service to party, parking fees
- valet service or parking fees
- venue
- videographer

Negotiating

Things to keep in mind when negotiating your event ...

- Day of the week – weekend events, especially during holiday weekends, tend to cost more than weekday events.

- Time of day – events held at night tend to cost more than events held during the day.

- Venue location – events held in bigger cities or in popular tourist areas will cost more.

- Number of guests – negotiating a better rate is often easier the higher the guest count.

- Food – negotiating too hard may affect the quality of the food. In general, a buffet is more expensive than a plated meal because portions are not easily controlled; however, the staff and service will be less.

- Bar – a consumption bar tends to be more affordable, unless your guests consume a lot of alcohol, when you will want an open bar. Consider the total number of guests, how many children there will be, the time of day and transportation adults will be taking.

- Number of staff – there should be at least one server for every 15 people and at least one bartender for every 50 to 75 people minimum – more staff means better service for your guests.

- Extra rooms – you may be able to get a picture room and/or changing rooms for free or at discounted rates.

Average Prices

Catering any party can be more or less expensive based on the season and competition all the vendors have, so consider:

Most popular times (which means less negotiating room) are Saturday nights in March, April, May, October, and November.

Less popular times (which means more negotiating room) are Sundays, Saturday afternoons, and some holidays.

Formally you can also "open the Torah" and celebrate on three days during the week and a few Jewish holidays. Your temple will direct you on this.

Average prices (many factors are involved): Lower-end prices will be available in the suburbs; major cities will have the higher-end prices.

- Catering: approximately two-thirds of the entire budget, usually, $75-200+ per adult and $25-50 per child plus tax and service charges. Many caterers bill for tipping so ask.
- Venue: $1,000-10,000. In-house catering may include room rental.
- Band DJ/ MC packages (dancers, lighting, screens): $3,500-12,000
- Photo booths: $800-1,500
- Other entertainment: $1,000-3,000
- Clothing: Service attire should cover shoulders and be business appropriate. Party attire is usually party formal, but anything goes.
- Tallit prices range from $65-400—Boys always have a tallit, girls sometimes have a tallit.
- Cake: $1.50-7.00 per slice (depending fillings, layers, design and size)
- Photography: $1,000-10,000+ per package (depending hourly rates, daily rates, size of albums, size of event, number of cameras, location, etc.)
- Videographer: $800-5,000 per package (depending number of cameras, number of people, number of copies, special effects, etc.)
- Montage: $500-1,000
- Limousines: 3-hour minimums, approximately $1,000
- Buses: 4 hour minimums, typically $500-1,000
- Planners: $155-6,000 per client (options: do-it-yourself, à la carte pricing, percentage of the event, dollar amount, etc.)

Sample Budget 1

Administration	Contract Company	Description/Notes	Estimated	Actual
Planner/Day of Director	Save the Date, LLC		$3,200.00	$ 3,200.00
Additional Day Of Planner			$0.00	$ 45.00
		Subtotal	$3,200.00	$ 3,245.00
Venue, Catering and				
Catering	Signature/Shalom	$57.95 a/$29.95k	$6,000.00	$ 8,485.60
Bar	kosher - by family		$300.00	$ 300.00
venue charges	Beth El		$1,650.00	$ 1,825.00
Guest Baskets			$200.00	$ 200.00
		Subtotal	$8,150.00	$ 10,810.60
Entertainment				
Band or DJ	Unique Dreams		$1,925.00	$ 1,925.00
photo booth	Pixilated	tinsel backdrop	$1,000.00	$ 1,068.00
games	Talk of the Town	casino, & more	$3,500.00	$ 3,708.35
		Subtotal	$6,425.00	$ 6,701.35
Photography and Video				
Photography			$2,400.00	$ 2,332.00
Videography			n/a	n/a
Montage			n/a	n/a
		Subtotal	$2,400.00	$ 2,332.00
Décor & Design				
Centerpieces			$600.00	$ 523.00
Logo			$100.00	$ 50.00
Decor		balloons suspended from	$1,500.00	$ 1,749.00
Stickers (80) & envelope				$ 90.00
		Subtotal	$2,200.00	$ 2,412.00
Rentals				
Spandex Tablecloths &			$850.00	$ 450.09
Uplights (bl&orange)			$300.00	$ 300.00
Security	Lare		$150.00	$ 100.00
Rentals	A Grand Event	(5) 4' tables & 10 (30" high)	$147.75	$ 243.26
		Subtotal	$1,447.75	$ 1,093.35
Favors and Retail				
Invitations			$700.00	$ 643.90
Favors	Bluetooth speakers		$500.00	$ 512.50
Favors	5 Blelow other kid gifts		$250.00	$ 250.00
Gift Cards	Amazon, Barnes & Noble,		$500.00	$ 500.00
Napkins (700)			$585.00	$ 258.20
Benchers (100)			$300.00	$ 209.00
kippot (100)			$300.00	$ 300.00
		Subtotal	$3,135.00	$ 2,673.60
		Event Total	**$26,957.75**	**$ 29,267.88**

Sample Budget 2

Administration	Contract Company	Description/Notes	Estimated	Actual
Planner/Day of Director	Save the Date, LLC	unlimited planning & day-of Director	$2,850.00	$2,850.00
		Subtotal	$2,850.00	$2,850.00
Venue, Catering and Lodging				
Catering	Bean Bag		$12,000.00	$12,100.00
misc. Catering			$2,500.00	$0.00
Bar			$1,800.00	$1,600.00
Venue charges	Beth Ami		$1,500.00	$1,000.00
Friday Night	Bean Bag		$2,000.00	$1,700.00
Hotel Costs		Hospitality Suite	$1,000.00	$700.00
Guest Baskets				
		Subtotal	$20,800.00	$17,100.00
Entertainment				
DJ & Zap Shots/screens	Unique Dreams	MC, zap shots/screens	$4,000.00	$3,895.00
Games, photo booth, green screen, other	Electric Entertainment	green screen, pop a shot	$1,500.00	$1,250.00
		Subtotal	$5,500.00	$5,145.00
Photography and Video				
Photography	Greg Land		$1,500.00	$1,500.00
Videography	FAS		$450.00	$425.00
Montage	Montagical		$400.00	$400.00
		Subtotal	$2,350.00	$2,325.00
Décor & Design				
Florist			n/a	n/a
Decor	Electric & STD		$3,000.00	$5,300.00
Logo	SAVE The DATE		$200.00	$75.00
		Subtotal	$3,200.00	$5,375.00
Rentals				
Lighting	SAVE The DATE		$300.00	$450.00
Linen	SAVE The DATE		$500.00	$650.00
Limousine/Transportation			$600.00	n/a
Security	Temple		$200.00	$250.00
		Subtotal	$1,600.00	$1,350.00
Attire				
Service/Party Attire			$1,000.00	$750.00
		Subtotal	$1,000.00	$750.00
Favors and Retail				
Save The Dates		email	$0.00	$0.00
Invitations/cards			$500.00	$700.00
Favors		knit hats	$1,000.00	$625.00
Napkins		unprinted	$600.00	$50.00
Guests Towels		unprinted	$300.00	$25.00
Place cards			$200.00	$137.50
kippot			$180.00	$215.00
		Subtotal	$2,780.00	$1,752.50
Day of				
Makeup/Hair			$250.00	$223.00
		Subtotal	$250.00	$223.00
		Event Total	**$40,330.00**	**$36,870.50**

Sample Budget 3

Administration	Contract Company	Description/Notes	Estimated	Actual
Planner/Day of Director	Save the Date, LLC	5 meetings & day-of	$2,175.00	$2,175.00
		Subtotal	$2,175.00	$2,175.00
Venue, Catering and Lodging				
Catering/Linens	Catering by Seasons		$15,000.00	$16,169.91
Bar	Old Line Liquors		$1,400.00	$1,345.89
Venue charges	VisArts	includes security	$4,500.00	$4,500.00
temple charges	Temple Emanuel		$500.00	$500.00
Friday Night	Gordon Biersch		$2,000.00	$1,700.00
Guest Baskets			$250.00	$200.00
		Subtotal	$23,650.00	$24,415.80
Entertainment				
Band or DJ	Washington Talent	MC Happy Feet	$5,500.00	$5,000.00
Games, photo booth, green screen, other	Washington Talent	Doodle Pix	$1,500.00	$1,378.00
		Subtotal	$7,000.00	$6,378.00
Photography and Video				
Photography	Cathy Gorey		$2,500.00	$1,800.00
Videography			n/a	n/a
Montage		homemade	$0.00	$0.00
		Subtotal	$2,500.00	$1,800.00
Décor & Design				
Florist			n/a	n/a
Decor			$2,000.00	$1,075.87
Logo			$200.00	$75.00
		Subtotal	$2,200.00	$1,150.87
Rentals				
Parking		validation cards	$300.00	$280.00
Rentals/Lighting	Cerfny		$5,000.00	$8,950.25
		Subtotal	$5,300.00	$9,230.25
Attire				
Service/Party Attire			$1,050.00	$825.00
		Subtotal	$1,050.00	$825.00
Favors and Retail				
Save The Dates			$0.00	$0.00
Invitations/thank notes	Carlson Craft	Quantity of 125	$700.00	$594.51
Favors		100 long sleeve ts & 135 cups w/ candy	$1,700.00	$2,281.18
Napkins/guest towels			n/a	n/a
Place cards		calligraphy on cups	$200.00	$100.00
kippots			$200.00	$180.00
		Subtotal	$2,800.00	$3,155.69
Day of				
Makeup/Hair		rehearsal & party	$550.00	$515.00
		Subtotal	$550.00	$515.00
		Event Total	**$47,225.00**	**$49,645.61**

Sample Budget 4

Administration	Contract Company	Description/Notes	Estimated	Actual
Planner/Day of Director	Save the Date, LLC	unlimited planning assistance & day-of	$4,200.00	$3,000.00
Additional Site Visit	SAVE the Date, LLC	2 hour meeting at decorator	$0.00	$300.00
Additional Staff Day of	SAVE the Date, LLC	3 person on-site for party	$0.00	$110.00
		Subtotal	$4,200.00	$3,410.00
Venue, Catering and Lodging				
Catering/Bar/Venue Charges	Woodmont Country Club	food/bar/staff/venue charges	$17,000.00	$28,727.33
misc. Catering	Mama's Donuts	donut holes for 150 guests	$650.00	$650.00
temple charges			$500.00	$475.00
Friday Night			$2,500.00	$2,380.00
Guest Baskets			$300.00	$260.00
		Subtotal	$20,950.00	$32,492.33
Entertainment				
Band or DJ	Washington Talent	MC Ali, zap shots	$7,000.00	$6,750.00
Games, photo booth, green screen, other	Carbone & TapSnap	airbrush tattoos, patch hats, tapsnap	$2,000.00	$3,503.20
		Subtotal	$9,000.00	$10,253.20
Photography and Video				
Photography	MBK Photography		$5,000.00	$4,300.00
Videography			n/a	n/a
Montage		done by friend	$0.00	$0.00
		Subtotal	$5,000.00	$4,300.00
Décor & Design				
Florist/Décor/Lighting/Linens	Davinci	includes lighting and linens	$18,000.00	$24,075.37
Logo			$200.00	$200.00
Envelope Box	STD	locked envelope box with logo inserts	$25.00	$25.00
Table Numbers	STD	custom reserved table numbers with logo	$13.00	$11.25
		Subtotal	$18,238.00	$24,311.62
Rentals				
Parking	Woodmont	3 Attendants/Valet	$250.00	$225.00
Security	Woodmont	4 security guards	$725.00	$700.00
Rentals	A Grand Event	13 high top tables	$0.00	$200.00
		Subtotal	$975.00	$1,125.00
Attire				
Service Attire			$1,500.00	$1,395.45
Party Attire			$4,000.00	$3,789.45
		Subtotal	$5,500.00	$5,184.90
Favors and Retail				
Invitations/Additional Cards		includes additional cards	$1,500.00	$2,100.00
Favors		long sleeve ts with laces	$2,000.00	$1,746.98
Other - Pillows	STD	8 custom double sided logo pillows	$275.00	$247.76
Napkins		1500 custom logo napkins	$500.00	$459.95
Guests Towels			$300.00	n/a
kippots			$250.00	$196.00
		Subtotal	$4,825.00	$4,750.69
Day of				
Makeup/Hair			$1,025.00	$932.18
other - Ice Sculpture	Hot Ice Inc.	3 bottle holder	$425.00	$418.70
		Subtotal	$1,450.00	$1,350.88
		Event Total	**$70,138.00**	**$87,178.62**

Vendor Tipping

DJ/Band
- $100-500   depending on the size of the band
- $50-125   main contact or MC
- $20-25 per   band members/dancers/DJ/electrician

> **TIP:** A rule of thumb is $100 for your main contact, usually the MC or the head of the band. How much extra has he/she done for you? How often have you spoken or met?

The In-house catering (in a hotel or restaurant for example) traditionally includes a tip/service charge in the bill, so this is extra:
- $20-25 per   wait staff/server/bartender/attendant (Coat or Bathroom)
- $50-200   captain/head waiter/chef
- $75-150   sales rep/in house contact/catering manager

Catering brought to a location is usually paid an hourly rate with a minimum, and the tip/service charge is usually not invoiced. Service Charge and Tip are not necessarily the same thing:
- $30-75 per   wait staff/server/bartender/attendant (Coat or Bathroom)
- $100-200   captain/head waiter/chef
- $75-150   sales rep/in house contact/catering manager

> **TIP:** A rule of thumb is to always ask your sales representative what is "usually" done.

Other tips you will want to budget are:
- $75-200   event Planner or 15 % of total fee for services
- $25-50   event planner assistant
- $50-100   janitor/volunteer at location
- $20-25 per   Valet – include a sign telling guests "Tip Taken Care Of"

> **TIP:** Others not generally tipped but at your discretion are:

- $50-200   photographer/videographer
- $50-100   photographer/videographer assistant
- $20-25 per   green screen/photobooth/other entertainment/security

An appropriate tip for the rabbi or cantor is a donation to their discretionary fund. Be sure to invite the cantor, rabbi, and tutor the celebration.

> **TIP:** A great gift/thank you to give all your vendors is a written online review.

Your Budget

Keep track of your budget as you plan your event.

SAVE The DATE, LLC events and promotions your way							
Administration	Contract Company	Description/Notes	Estimated	Actual	1st payment	2nd payment	3rd Payment	Amount
Planner/Day of Director	Save the Date, LLC							
		Subtotal	$0.00	$0.00	$0.00	$0.00	$0.00	$0.00
Venue, Catering & Lodging								
Catering								
misc. Catering								
Cake								
Bar								
Venue charges								
temple charges								
Friday Night								
Hotel Costs								
Guest Baskets								
		Subtotal	$0.00	$0.00	$0.00	$0.00	$0.00	$0.00
Entertainment								
Band or DJ								
Games, photo booth, green screen, other								
		Subtotal	$0.00	$0.00	$0.00	$0.00	$0.00	$0.00
Photography & Video								
Photography								
Videography								
Montage								
		Subtotal	$0.00	$0.00	$0.00	$0.00	$0.00	$0.00
Décor & Design								
Florist								
Decor								
Logo								
		Subtotal	$0.00	$0.00	$0.00	$0.00	$0.00	$0.00
Rentals								
Lighting								
Linen								
Limousine								
Parking								
Security								
		Subtotal	$0.00	$0.00	$0.00	$0.00	$0.00	$0.00
Attire								
Service Attire								
Party Attire								
Misc.								
		Subtotal	$0.00	$0.00	$0.00	$0.00	$0.00	$0.00
Favors & Retail								
Save The Dates								
Invitations/Cards								
Programs								
Favors								
Other								
Napkins/Guest Towels								
Place cards								
kippots								
		Subtotal	$0.00	$0.00	$0.00	$0.00	$0.00	$0.00
Day of								
Hair								
Travel								
other								
misc. food								
		Subtotal	$0.00	$0.00	$0.00	$0.00	$0.00	$0.00
		Event Total	**$0.00**	**$0.00**	**$0.00**	**$0.00**	**$0.00**	**$0.00**

SECTION 3: EVENT PLANNER

Why should you hire a party planner? If you want to have fun planning your event, consider hiring a planner who:

- gets you discounts and better prices
- is educated and continues educating themselves about the event and the religious community
- already has a working relationship with vendors
- has pull with everyone and maintains connections
- helps you stay organized
- is involved in associations in the industry
- is there to assist all the vendors
- is responsive to stressful times or issues
- keeps all our paperwork
- puts out "fires"
- reminds you of what is popular now
- teaches you what to do
- tells you what is "traditional," yet helps you to keep an open mind
- understands the process because he/she is Jewish and has personally been through the process
- will always be there for anything YOU need or want; stays on your side
- uses years of knowledge

Your venue or caterer may be willing to help you plan, but remember their focus is the location and/or the food service; an independent planner is there for just your needs. The more creative you want to be, the more you may need a planner to help you pull everything together.

Party Planner Info Sheet

Basic Information

    Company:

    Contact person:

    Phone:

    E-mail:

    Cell:

    Fax:

    Address:

Contract and Payment

    Total hours:

    Total contract:

    Contract signed:

    Total charges:

    Deposit amount:

        Due:

        Payment: Credit card

                            Check (check #:   )

    Final Payment amount:

        Due:

        Payment: Credit card

                            Check (check #:   )

"Day of" Director

Why hire a "Day of" Director?

If you want to have fun and be a guest at your party, consider hiring a "day of" person to:

- Assist with the sign-in book by making sure it is set up and guests sign it
- Additional eyes on everything
- Be in charge while you are relaxing or at temple
- Be there for anything that you need
- Check in all vendors
- Check on all the bathrooms
- Check on all the tables
- Call cabs if needed
- Contact all the vendors at event to keep them on "day of" schedule
- Deal with emergencies
- Direct the clean-up after the event
- Keep all the paperwork
- Let you be a guest at your party
- Pack up your car or hotel room after the party, so you can make sure you leave with everything that belongs to you
- Provide additional security/keep an eye on kids
- Provide emergency "box" (items in case of minor to extreme emergencies)
- Put out "fires"
- Set up
- Sew and fix anything that needs fixing
- Take care of your family (make sure you get photo booth pics, food and drink, etc.)
- Much more…

How many directors will you need?
- at least one for parties of 125 guests
- an assistant to the director for parties with more than 125 guests
- another assistant when more than 45 guests are young

What to give to your day of director:
- All vendors' contact information
- Alphabetical list of guests and table assignments
- Any special instructions
- Box A and Box B lists
- Logo – pdf, jpg and other formats
- Clearly defined layout(s) and diagram(s)
- Copies of all contracts and addendums to the contracts
- Copies of all speeches
- Copy of Candle Lighting Ceremony
- Final payments and tips in identified/labeled envelopes
- Invitation for photographer and videographer
- Layout and seating lists
- List of set-up items
- List of what to pack in what car (centerpieces, gifts, decorations, etc.)
- Photo list
- Place cards in alphabetical order by last name
- Special meal requirements
- Specify colors of napkins and linens
- Specific information
  - Your drink(s) of choice for the party
  - Any important information
  - Misc. décor
- The schedules - long and short (see schedule section)
- Your cell phone number

Day-of Director Info Sheet

Basic Information

    Company:

    Contact person:

    Phone:

    E-mail:

    Cell:

    Fax:

    Address:

Contract and Payment

    Total hours:

    Total contract:

    Contract signed:

    Total charges:

    Deposit amount:

        Due:

            Payment: Credit card

                           Check (check #:   )

    Final Payment amount:

        Due:

            Payment: Credit card

                           Check (check #:   )

SECTION 4: TEMPLE AND RELIGION

Friday night temple services:

- Friday night services generally consist of regular temple members and immediate family of the Mitzvah child who are in town for the weekend.

- Many temples involve the Mitzvah children into the Friday night services. Consider attending with your close family and friends to get into the spirit of the event.

- There is usually an "out-of-towners" or Sabbath dinner with family and friends before or after Friday services.

You are not obligated to feed your guests all weekend. In fact, some guests prefer to be on their own for part of the weekend. Alternatives to a big dinner might be:

- Host a "hospitality" room with snacks and drinks to offer a meeting place for guests.

- Host a late-night dessert party. This gives your immediate family more relaxing time, and you still get to see your guests before the big day.

Saturday morning temple services:

- All invited guests, adults, and children attend the temple at your child's service time.

- You generally place kippot for your guests outside the sanctuary. Attach your child's invitation to the kippah basket or on a stand next to your kippot so your guests take your kippot and the shared family or non-guest-Temple members (hopefully) notice that these particular kippot are for your event.

- Generally, you provide and/or pay for an oneg or Kiddush following a service. An oneg consists of light pastries and drinks for anyone who attends Temple that day.

- You may choose to provide an "extended" oneg, a more substantial luncheon foods only for your guests.

- Some temples require you to pay for an extended oneg for everyone in attendance so check the rules and adjust your budget accordingly.

- For extended onegs, you may want to decorate with plants or simple centerpieces.

- If you are having a luncheon party at another location, you should provide transportation for any children who attend services.

Havdalah Services are at "the close of the Sabbath" or in the afternoon.

- The same rules apply for am and pm services—the main difference is that you should provide transportation for young guests to get from the temple to the party if you are having celebrations immediately following.

- An extended oneg/Kiddush is generally not held after a havdalah service.

- A havdalah set may be necessary for you to provide during a Havdalah service.

Children and friend letters are helpful about how to behave and "dress" and act at this Jewish event—both at temple and at the party. The letter would note pick up times for children at the end of the party for their safety and your responsibility towards them. It may also have information about being respectful and services, putting away cell phones, dressing appropriately (generally business formal/covered shoulders and age appropriate) and information about transportation being provided from the temple.

Temple Information Sheet

Basic Information

    Company:

    Contact person:

    Phone:

    E-mail:

    Cell:

    Fax:

    Address:

Contract and Payment

    Total hours:

    Total contract:

    Contract signed:

    Total charges:

    Deposit amount:

        Due:

            Payment: Credit card

                          Check (check #:   )

    Final Payment amount:

        Due:

            Payment: Credit card

                          Check (check #:   )

Temple Décor

Basic Information

    Company:

    Contact person:

    Phone:

    E-mail:

    Cell:

    Fax:

    Address:

Contract and Payment

    Total hours:

    Total contract:

    Contract signed:

    Total charges:

    Deposit amount:

        Due:

        Payment: Credit card

                          Check (check #:   )

    Final Payment amount:

        Due:

        Payment: Credit card

                          Check (check #:   )

Temple Oneg/Kiddush Information Sheet

Basic Information

    Company:

    Contact person:

    Phone:

    E-mail:

    Cell:

    Fax:

    Address:

Contract and Payment

    Total hours:

    Total contract:

    Contract signed:

    Total charges:

    Deposit amount:

        Due:

        Payment: Credit card

                        Check (check #:   )

    Final Payment amount:

        Due:

        Payment: Credit card

                        Check (check #:   )

Aliyah

An aliyah is an honor or "responsibility" given to friends, family, and parents.
- ✦ Your temple has particular temple's rules for aliyah: some allow a limited number of aliyahs.
- ✦ Some temples require a donation for each aliyah.
- ✦ You may offer these different honors to individuals at the celebration

You will need the Hebrew and English names of anyone who will be performing an aliyah, as well as the Hebrew and English names of those same individuals' parents.

Temple aliyahs include:
- ✦ opening the Ark
- ✦ closing the Ark
- ✦ reading from the Torah
- ✦ singing before/after Torah readings
- ✦ holding the Torah
- ✦ "dressing"/"undressing" the Torah
- ✦ presenting of the tallis

Honors at the celebration include:
- ✦ Ha-Motzi over challah
- ✦ Ha-Motzi over wine
- ✦ Speeches
- ✦ Brucha
- ✦ Help with arrangements
- ✦ Paying for the brunch or Shabbat dinner

Mitzvah Project

Mitzvah projects are not "required" by most temples because becoming a Bar/Bat Mitzvah is about reading from the Torah not necessarily about doing a mitzvah. Today we always try to incorporate Mitzvah projects for a deeper reason. Becoming Bar/Bat Mitzvah in today's world we want our children to "understand" the type of person we are and we want to be. We want to teach them about doing good deeds and we want them to feel that this time in their life is not just about a party or about learning a language that they may never use, but it is about becoming a "good Jew" in today's world and continuing to be that same person in the future. It also is a mitzvah to show you have taken these steps to the guests who are joining you in this milestone.

Some Mitzvah ideas can based on your child's interests, your Torah or haftorah portion
or a family mission:

- Ask guests to bring slightly used items that you will deliver to the needy
- Donations of needed items
- Donations to any Jewish organizations
- Favors, such as adopt an animal, plant a tree, etc.
- Organize fundraisers for non-profit organizations
- Pay for children's' Mitzvahs at an Israeli orphanage
- Raise awareness of any cause
- Spend time at animal shelters—donations for cages
- Spend time with the elderly
- Throw birthday parties at homeless shelters
- Wish list donations

Your Rabbi, computer, and Jewish organizations are great resources for Mitzvah ideas.

The Mitzvah Project may be highlighted in the invitation, on a poster with photos of your child at the location and a sample of what you made or purchased and displayed as décor. Some prefer it is only mentioned in your speech and others continue to call attention to the cause at the celebration, for example in the candle lighting ceremony.

Candle Lighting Ceremony

In my personal opinion, the candle lighting is a means to an end. Speaking in front of your peers at 13 years of age is not easy. Candle lighting assists your child(ren) in welcoming, acknowledging and honoring their guests. A pre-prepared speech, poster, or traditional candelabra eases the process because they have something to do with their hands and a "cheat sheet." It is also a way to get a photo of each group of important people who will take part in the ceremony. Finally, it is a way to make this event more than just a party; it now becomes meaningful.

What is a candle lighting ceremony?

- A traditional candle lighting is a 14-holder candelabra (1 for good luck)

- The Mitzvah child reads a "poem," which invites guests to come up to the dance floor and light a candle in their own honor

- Generally, there is a song to go along with each person or group of guests invited to come up, typically, a family or group of friends

- Take a photo of each group with the Mitzvah child.

- Usually, the Mitzvah child lights a candle in honor of someone's memory.

There are no rules, no book on "how to observe a Mitzvah," so this ceremony can be short, creative, interesting, involve all attendees, or be replaced with a totally different concept.

The Cup of Life Ceremony is a great way to change up a candle lighting ceremony – it is done with wine and cups. Incorporating mitzvah projects, art and themes are also great modern versions of the candle lighting concept.

Use the internet and make this a unique experience for your child.

Shabbat Dinner

What do you do for the Shabbat dinner?
- Out-of-town guests should be invited to the Shabbat dinner and, if it is in your budget, you may choose to include immediate and extended family

- Another option is to have a nice family dinner after Friday night services at your home, a restaurant, or the hotel where all your guests are staying.

- Don't feel like you must feed the out of town guests the night before, some guests appreciate the time to visit the area, see relatives, or relax on a precious weekend.

- Consider a dessert get together.

- Don't forget your camera, you will want the memories.

- Consider simple decorations then donate the centerpieces/flowers to a nearby retirement home or another location that could use the centerpiece.

- Decoration ideas: potted plants, flowers, an item purchased from an organization that gives a percentage of the proceeds to a charity, candles, or donation baskets.

- If you chose to do a small family dinner, maybe have the dinner early so it is before temple. Then offer a hospitality suite at the hotel for your out-of-towners. Join them in the hospitality suite for snacks and a light dessert after temple so you start the weekend visiting with friends and family.

Shabbat Dinner Information Sheet

Basic Information

    Company:

    Contact person:

    Phone:

    E-mail:

    Cell:

    Fax:

    Address:

Contract and Payment

    Total hours:

    Total contract:

    Contract signed:

    Total charges:

    Deposit amount:

        Due:

        Payment: Credit card

                          Check (check #:   )

    Final Payment amount:

        Due:

        Payment: Credit card

                          Check (check #:   )

SECTION 5: YOUR VENUE

Your venue will determine your experience and your costs, so take the time to do the research and have fun; it won't be long before your 13 year old is graduation and considering marriage. This experience is not unique to our lives, so take a friend along and bounce ideas off each other!

Choosing a venue:
- Make appointments to visit only those venues that have the space for your event and the availability you need.

- Collect menus, layouts, and an equipment list from the venues you visit.

- If possible, take pictures of the space(s) you are interested in when you visit each venue: including the lobby, the bathrooms, furniture, etc. so you can remember the pros and cons as you make decisions.

Booking a venue:
- Some venues will only book an event one year or less in advance.

- If you have not received a contract within approximately two weeks of your booking conversation, call the venue to inquire about the status.

- Carefully review the contract then sign it and return it quickly. Double check the date and time - take note of any minimums and/or required number guarantees.

- Typically you will be asked to provide a security deposit and/or a credit card number to hold the space.

Your on-site event manager or contact person may change before your event -- you are "buying" the location, not the event manager.

Questions to Ask and Things to Consider

For catering and food service:
- Is outside catering allowed at the venue? Does the venue have a list of pre-approved caterers?
- If the venue is providing china, silverware, and stemware and can you see it ahead of time?
- Are the kitchen facilities adequate for your event?
- What food service can they provide? How many servers per table will be provided?
- How many bars will be available to you? How many bartenders will be provided?
- How will the bar be set up? Will it be an open, consumption, or a cash bar?
- Is premium liquor available? At what charge?
- If the venue is catering your event, will they provide a cake? If you must provide your own cake, can the venue refrigerate the cake if necessary? Will there be a cutting fee?
- Are there any special meal options (*vegetarian, kosher, etc.*)?
- Is there a fee for liquor you provide (corkage fee)? What is the policy about unopened bottles that you provide?
- Can the venue provide meals for your vendors? Is it possible to receive these meals at a discounted cost?

For vendors:
- What time will your vendors be allowed to set up your event and when must they break it down?
- Where will your vendors enter the venue?
- Where will your vendors be able to park? Will they be charged for parking? Can vouchers be provided for them?
- Does the venue offer meals for your vendors? Can you get a discount for these meals?
- Will the venue store anything overnight for your vendors? At what fee?

For your event:
- What are the time slots for your event?
- Is there another event at the venue before and/or after your event? If so, will there be any conflicts?
- What areas will be available for you to use (a single room, multiple rooms, outdoor areas, etc.)?

If you are considering an outdoor area, what are the inclement weather policies? Can the venue provide you with indoor areas to use?

© SAVE *The* DATE, LLC EVENTS
events and promotions your way
WWW.SaveTheDateLLCEvents.com

- What is included in your rental fee (table sizes and quantities, chairs, dance floor, lighting, linens, a cake, etc.)? Request quantities, sizes, and colors.
- Is there a coat room for guests? Can it be used to store any gifts?
- Can the venue provide tables for your event? If so, what are the size options?
- Can the venue provide linens for your event? If so, what are the linen options?
- Can the venue provide chairs and/or other seating arrangements (such as couches)? What color and style are the seating options? If possible, take pictures of the rooms.
- When can rentals (tables, chairs, linens, etc.) be delivered to the venue? Where should all of the rentals be delivered? To a specific person, a loading dock, by certain times? When must rentals be picked up by?
- What parking arrangements does the venue offer (valet, self-park, free parking, paid parking, indoor, outdoor, etc.)? If guests must pay for parking, can the venue bill you and provide vouchers for guests?
- By what time must the venue be vacated after your event?

General venue information:
- What is the maximum number of people the venue can accommodate for your event?
- Can the venue accommodate younger children?
- What licenses does the venue hold -- health department licenses? Liquor licenses, etc.?
- What is the policy about a security deposit? Gratuities for staff?
- Is dancing allowed? Is alcohol?
- Is outside catering allowed at the venue?
- Are decorations allowed? What are the guidelines or limitations?
- Where are the bathrooms?
- Are changing rooms available? Free or at a fee?
- Is there adequate parking?
- Does the venue have heating and/or air-conditioning?
- Does the venue put up holiday decorations that will be there on the night of your event?

The venue and your vendors will need basic information from you, so it may be helpful to create a "profile" that you can send to everyone. See the page at the end of this section for an example. You should include:

- Your contact information – your name, the name of the honoree, address, home and cell phone numbers, fax number and e-mail. If you are using a planner, provide the venue with your planner's information as well.

© SAVE The DATE, LLC EVENTS
events and promotions your way
WWW.SaveTheDateLLCEvents.com

- Date and time of the event -- only provide alternate dates if you are specifically asked, as it may lessen the availability of your original date.
- Type of event.
- Approximate number of people you are expecting. Remember that the holidays, location, and travel requirements of your event changes your turnout.
- Number of younger children you are expecting, if any.
- Special needs or accommodations for your guests, including kosher, that some vendors may not assume.
- Outside catering information, if available.
- Vendor information, if available.
- Contracts (see contract section in catering)

Questions to Ask at Initial Site Inspection

- ✦ TAKE PHOTOGRAPHS OF ALL THE SPACES
- ✦ REQUEST A LAYOUT FROM VENUE

What is the square footage of the space?	
Where is the loading dock?	
Maximum Number of Guests - Fire Code?	
Where are the fire exits? Request a layout that shows them.	
What is provided/available/included in the contract? i.e. linens (colors), plates, chairs (type/color), tables (size/shape), etc. Request list	
Are there any restrictions? i.e. Red Wine, Candles, Chocolate Fountain, etc.	
What type of flooring? If rug, what color?	
Where is cocktail hour? Are there multiple Options?	
What is the size of the dance floor? Is it included? Is a Stage included?	
Is there a built Bar? What are the bar Options?	
How Does the lighting work in the room? Is is separate or all attached? Any special lighting options?	
Are there any planned renovations? Will we be informed if a renovation is to occur?	

Are Holiday Decorations on our date? What do they look like?	
What happens if you lose Flag or Change Names? Will we be informed? can we change contract?	
Will there be any holiday decorations up? Can it be removed?	
Who is our Primary Contact?	
Who is our Secondary Contact?	

Considering the Outdoors

Planning an outdoor Bar/Bat Mitzvah can be a rewarding challenge. Does the site require:
- tents for potential rain? At what cost?
- any additional tents for the caterer? Where?
- do guests and staff have to work around slopes or steps?
- does it allow hard flooring for dancing and level walking, especially for the elderly?
- ramps?
- more staff for an outdoor event?

Utilities:
- is there electrical?
- is there water? How much and what kind?
- is there a place for garbage?

Menu:
- will nature will affect the quality of your foods? For example, chocolate fountains and some cakes should not be on any outdoor menu.
- usually anything cooked inside can be done outside; some caterers bring prepared food to the site.
- you may have a menu that includes grilling or active stations outdoors.
- tents with sides block the wind so delicate food may not be affected.

Light and Heat:
- what are the lighting options for evenings?
- what are the heating options? Heat lamps for cool weather?
- what are the air options? Fans for hot days?

Nature:
- will birds or droppings be a hazard?
- in the woods, consider animals, protecting food from leaves, mosquitoes and bugs.
- consider traps with sweet solutions, not insecticide

Request for Proposal (RFP)

To vendor: Today's Date:

Contact Information:
    Name/s:
    Honoree name:
    Telephone:
    Cell:
    Email:
    Address:
    Fax:

Preferred Date:

Alternative Date:

Service(s) Needed:

Time:

    Type of event:

    Preferred time:

    Number of guests:

    Ceremony location:

    Number of celebration rooms for event:

    Number of sleeping rooms:

    Food and Beverage Requirement/Budget:

Audio Visual Requirement:
    Other:

    Please send menu information to:

We hope to hear from you by _____.
Thank you.

© **SAVE The DATE, LLC EVENTS**
events and promotions your way
WWW.SaveTheDateLLCEvents.com

Venue Information Sheet

Basic Information

    Company:

    Contact person:

    Phone:

    E-mail:

    Cell:

    Fax:

    Address:

Contract and Payment

    Total hours:

    Total contract:

    Contract signed:

    Total charges:

    Deposit amount:

        Due:

            Payment: Credit card

                          Check (check #:   )

    Final Payment amount:

        Due:

            Payment: Credit card

                          Check (check #:   )

SECTION 6: CATERING

Planning your catering:
- You may need to get permission from the venue to use an outside caterer.
- Schedule a meeting with your on-site catering or banquet manager.
- Make sure your catering manager can accommodate your budget and understands your expectations and needs.
- Schedule a tasting for approximately 1-2 months before your event.
- Create an event schedule for your catering manager and/or the chef to ensure that your food will be served as you expect it to be -- be very specific.
- Ask about cancellation and weather-emergency policies and fees.
- Keep in mind that tax and gratuities/service charges are not included in most catering proposals but may appear on the final bill. If gratuity is not included on the final bill, you are responsible for determining and providing the tip(s).

Catering suggestions:
- Consider serving a "mixed plate" that offers two types of meat.
- When choosing a menu, remember that special meals may have different pricings and may need to be ordered ahead of time (vegetarian, kosher, children's meals, etc.).
- Consider ordering a less expensive meal or sandwiches for your vendors to eat in a separate room or space during a break.
- If your banquet/on-site manager has exceeded your expectations, consider offering extra gratuity (anywhere from $50 and up).
- Plan what you would like to do with the leftover food after your event. Many hotels and caterers do not allow food to be taken out of the hotel or event.

Contract

Your catering and venue contracts should include:

- The date and time of your event

- The room and the policy about switching rooms

- What is included with your rental fee (tables, chairs, linens, a dance floor, lighting, etc.)

- Any minimums, for example, how many meals you pay for regardless of how many guests show up and eat

- The type of food service you will receive – the food and number of servers, if a buffet how long it will remain open, bar service and liquor brands, etc.

- The pricing breakdown – security deposit, room rental, food and bar services and staff, parking, gratuities, taxes, overtime, etc.

- A payment schedule

- The due date for a final guest count

- The name of your current planner and the on-site, "day of" event manager

- Vendor policies like set up and break down times, storage, any break room and food for the vendors, etc.

- Any insurance, change of ownership/name, inclement weather and Force Majeure policies.

- Other policies like restrictions on decorations and outside catering, etc.

- Ask about holiday decorations

- Anything you negotiated with the venue

- Closing policies

Catering Information Sheet

Basic Information

    Company:

    Contact person:

    Phone:

    E-mail:

    Cell:

    Fax:

    Address:

Contract and Payment

    Total hours:

    Total contract:

    Contract signed:

    Total charges:

    Deposit amount:

        Due:

            Payment: Credit card

                         Check (check #:   )

    Final Payment amount:

        Due:

            Payment: Credit card

                         Check (check #:   )

Cake

Basic Information

    Company:

    Contact person:

    Phone:

    E-mail:

    Cell:

    Fax:

    Address:

Contract and Payment

    Total hours:

    Total contract:

    Contract signed:

    Total charges:

    Deposit amount:

        Due:

            Payment: Credit card

                            Check (check #:   )

    Final Payment amount:

        Due:

            Payment: Credit card

                            Check (check #:   )

Celebrate with Food, Dancing and Drink

There are many ways to cut back on bar expenses and still have a great time:
- select a venue where you can purchase your own alcohol
- make sure staff only opens bottles as needed: stores will take back unopened bottles
- provide beer and wine not hard liquor
- provide limited alcohol with a menu on the bar
- for daytime parties, consider per drink/by consumption pricing
- in the evening, consider your guests when deciding on open bar or per drink pricing

TIP: At most events, guests will take a drink, put it down and sometimes not finish it. It gets watery or they lose it so they will get another.

Bar options:
- premium/platinum – all major high-end brands
- call – medium brands
- rail – house brands
- white bar – soda, wine and beer
- Purchase your own or let the caterer/venue handle it.

If you are purchasing your own:
- ask your caterer to provide the accompaniments (cherries, limes, ice, mixers, etc.).
- consider letting the caterer handle the ice, bar amenities, glasses and coffee.
- asks liquor stores to deliver and arranges for someone to take back unused items (they won't take back beer out of a larger pack and wet labels).
- asks your caterer how much and what to purchase.

A caring host:
- always uses a legal, certified bartender serving and watching the bar
- provides different glasses for alcoholic drinks so children's drinks stand out.
- considers some fun nonalcoholic beverages.
- does not allow bartenders to display money or tip jars (guests should never have to open their pockets, purses, or wallets).
- closes the bar 30 minutes before the party ends
- tells all staff that anyone who looks as though they cannot drive should not drive: arrangements should be made or a cab called.

Bar

Basic Information

    Company:

    Contact person:

    Phone:

    E-mail:

    Cell:

    Fax:

    Address:

Contract and Payment

    Total hours:

    Total contract:

    Contract signed:

    Total charges:

    Deposit amount:

        Due:

        Payment: Credit card

                          Check (check #:   )

    Final Payment amount:

        Due:

        Payment: Credit card

                          Check (check #:   )

SECTION 7: ENTERTAINMENT

The new trend is to have a combination of a band and a DJ, or an MC who can sing. Before you decide what you and your child prefer, consider:

- How much you do you want the band or DJ to interact with your guests and what kind of interaction you expect - *games, requests, etc.?*
- What attire will you want for the band or DJ? What will be appropriate for your occasion and your guests?
- Will you provide food for the band, DJ/MC and other performers?
- Will you have special songs? Are you willing to pay the band to learn them?

In choosing a band or DJ:
- Review videotaped performances of any bands or DJs that interest you. Keep in mind that the sound may be slightly distorted in the video.
- If possible watch the band or DJ perform and *if you are allowed to; watch part of the performance at someone else's event, dress properly for the occasion and only stay for a short time.*
- When watching a band or DJ perform, pay attention to things like style, timing, tone, and volume.
- Observe the audience as the band or DJ is performing. Do people seem to be enjoying the performance?
- How does the band or DJ handle breaks? Will there be other entertainment during these breaks? Are there extra fees for a break-free performance?
- Make sure the name of the band or DJ is not overly featured at the event or on the equipment

When you have selected a candidate, ask:
- Does the band leader or DJ/MC understand your ideas and expectations for the entertainment you desire?
- Can this band play my must-play list? Have they played mitzvahs?
- Does your venue have the equipment/space/lighting/electricity this band needs?
- Who will be the band leader, band members, DJ or MC?
- When can the name(s) be put into the contract?
- What happens if someone becomes unavailable at a later time?

Your Music Selections

Your music should be a reflection of you, your child and your family, so do give suggestions to your musical act, but they need the final decisions as they will feel out your crowd.
- Although it is a child-centered party, remember that children love adult music and adults love the music from when they were young.
- Classics are always great picks.
- Special songs are fun: a basketball-centric song for a basketball theme; a song with your child's name in it; a theme song for the party, a special song for the guest(s) coming up to light the candle.

Our must-play list is:

_____

Our preferred play list is:

_____

Our do not play list is:

_____

Our list for grand entrance songs is:

_____

Our list for candle lighting songs is:

_____

Discuss the program with your musical entertainment and go over your guest list so they are prepared.

Band/MC/DJ Information Sheet

Basic Information

    Company:

    Contact person:

    Phone:

    E-mail:

    Cell:

    Fax:

    Address:

Contract and Payment

    Total hours:

    Total contract:

    Contract signed:

    Total charges:

    Deposit amount:

        Due:

            Payment: Credit card

                           Check (check #:   )

    Final Payment amount:

        Due:

            Payment: Credit card

                           Check (check #:   )

Fun and Games

Photo fun is the most popular "other form" of entertainment because games keep many guests busy and allows everyone to take home memories. You can receive a USB flash drive of all of the fun photos and new technologies make this a great add-on at minimal expense. Companies have many forms of photo fun including frames, green screen, key chains, photo scopes, sunglasses and even photos on sports balls that can double as place cards on the tables, a real conversation starter.

Games and other activities can be run by the MC/DJ or hired entertainment (casino, game show, sports). Prizes are a way to keep kids participating and themes based on the Mitzvah project add a dimension to the fun and leave a keepsake to take home. A new 10 second slow motion video, nail art, and washable tattoos are popular.

Other entertainment:
- airbrush artist
- art projects
- caricaturist
- carnival games
- casino
- community service projects like making bag lunches for the local home as part of the children's activities, or stuffing goodie-bags as a cocktail hour project? Or writing soldiers letters to replace "hired" entertainers?
- competitive games
- dancing - boys will dance less without girls, but girls alone may still dance. So, keep them entertained in other ways because you are responsible!
- demonstrations
- game show
- hair braiding
- interactive entertainment
- karaoke
- live entertainment
- money machines
- photo centers
- robots
- sport-based games
- t-shirt screening
- theme entertainment

Actors as Entertainment

Adding actors in costume can add "fluff." Table acts, party starters, and directional actors expect high pay, a green room, changing rooms and meals or water, but they:

- make conversation
- act a part
- start conversations
- aid the theme

Some roles played by actors:
- Airplane pilots
- Basketball players
- Check-in desk attendants
- Cheerleaders
- Dancers
- Dancing/singing rabbis
- Dracula
- Look-alikes
- Mixologists
- People in the news

Actor(s) Information Sheet

Basic Information

    Company:

    Contact person:

    Phone:

    E-mail:

    Cell:

    Fax:

    Address:

Contract and Payment

    Total hours:

    Total contract:

    Contract signed:

    Total charges:

    Deposit amount:

        Due:

        Payment: Credit card

                        Check (check #:   )

    Final Payment amount:

        Due:

        Payment: Credit card

                        Check (check #:   )

SECTION 8: PHOTOGRAPHY/VIDEOGRAPHY

When choosing your photographer, ask at least these questions:
- Does the photographer have a registered photography business?
- Does the photographer belong to any professional associations?
- Does the photographer have references or a portfolio? Check references and review a recent portfolio of an entire event.
- Does the photographer have insurance to protect both the client and him/herself and any employees?
- Does the photographer charge by the hour? stay on-site for the entire event?
- How and when is payment expected?
- How long has the photographer been in business?
- What is the photographer's education and experience in photography?
- What are the prices for additional photographs not included in any package?
- Which videographers has the photographer worked with?
- What will happen if the photographer becomes unavailable due to extenuating and/or unforeseen circumstances?

Equipment options:
- Does the photographer have emergency back-ups or replacements?
- What type(s) of camera(s) does the photographer use?
- What type(s) of lighting does the photographer use?

Photography options:
- Can the photographer take panoramic photographs? At what charge?
- Do you receive a CD of all the photographs from your event?
- Does the photographer touch up photographs? At what charge?
- Does the photographer develop and/or print photographs in-house?
- Does the photographer work with an on-site assistant?
- Does the photographer take black-and-white photographs?
- Does the photographer bring lighting and background for stills?
- What are the options for albums (colors, styles, leather, personalization, etc.)?
- Will you be able to view your photographs on a website after your event? When?
- Will the photographer retain the copyright of your photographs? Will he/she sign a copyright waiver?

Your event:
- After your event, when will you receive proofs?
Can you purchase the proofs and/or negatives?

- Does the photographer provide proofs on a CD?
- Has the photographer had experience at your type of event?
- Has the photographer had experience at your venue(s)? If not, will there be a site visit? At what charge?
- How long does it take after reviewing the proofs and choosing photographs for you to receive your album?
- Will the photographer contract another event the same day?
- Will the photographer take the photographs or send an associate?
- Will the photographer take photographs on the bima the day before the B'nai Mitzvah? At what charge?
- Will the photographer notify you before removing your proofs and/or negatives from his/her files?

Be sure to discuss what photos to take and what comes in a package. You may want to see portfolios of past events with the following essential pictures.

Ceremony/bima photographs of the honoree:
- reading the Torah (with the pointer)
- standing
- sitting
- the Ark by itself
- the family at their seats
- the honoree opening the Ark
- with parents
- with siblings
- with grandparents (mother's side, father's side, both sides)
- with the rabbi and cantor

The honoree:
- in front of a stained glass window
- outside and in front of the synagogue and/or reception
- with family outside and in front of the synagogue and/or reception venue
- with immediate family
- with parents
- with siblings
- with immediate family with grandparents (mother's side, father's side, both sides)
- with the immediate family with other close family (aunts, uncles, cousins)
- with best friends, neighbors, sorority/fraternity friends, etc.

Remember that you and your family will be busy and the day will be a blur. The honoree will not see everything and will miss much of what happens, so your photographs will want to include the traditional photos you always take (the three brothers from your dad's side, etc.) at any family reunion. A photographer needs the personality and wit to gather people kindly without interfering with the esprit de corps in a mix of posed or all candid photos.

Reception photographs:
- the reception room set out before guests arrive
- introductions at the reception
- the candle lighting ceremony
- the challah
- the horah
- various groups of friends (friends from the neighborhood, school, teams, Hebrew school classes, etc.)

Miscellaneous photographs:
- cake
- decorations (balloons, ice sculptures, etc.)
- the honoree's entrance into the reception
- favors
- place card table
- reception entrance(s)/door(s)
- sign-in board/book
- synagogue entrance
- tables/centerpieces

Photography Information Sheet

Basic information

    Company:

    Contact person:

    Phone:

    E-mail:

    Cell:

    Fax:

    Address:

Contract and Payment

    Total hours:

    Total contract:

    Contract signed:

    Total charges:

    Deposit amount:

        Due:

        Payment: Credit card

                           Check (check #:   )

    Final Payment amount:

        Due:

        Payment: Credit card

                           Check (check #:   )

Videography

Before hiring a videographer, find out if videotaping is allowed during the service. Ask for a demo and references.

- *What makes a videographer more expensive?*
  - Including guest interviews or stories in your video.
  - The equipment that can/will be used for your event.
  - The videographer's experience, specifically if he/she has experience at your venue(s) and at mitzvahs.
  - What you want in your final package, examples include: edited, unedited, or highlights.

- important shots you would like videotaped:
  - during the ceremony:
    - Ark
    - bima
    - congregation
    - outside of the synagogue
    - reading the Torah

  - during the reception:
    - cake
    - decorations, significant or favorite like balloons and ice sculptures
    - favors
    - Important moments (introductions, the candle lighting ceremony, the hora, etc.)
    - outside of the reception location
    - place card table
    - reception entrance(s)/door(s)
    - sign-in board/book
    - tables/centerpieces

  - people during the ceremony and reception:
    - close family (aunts, uncles, cousins, grandparents etc.)
    - honoree
    - individual comments/messages
    - parents
    - siblings
    - specific friends

This has been done before, your SAVE The DATE planner will help with this process.

Videography Information Sheet

Basic Information

    Company:

    Contact person:

    Phone:

    E-mail:

    Cell:

    Fax:

    Address:

Contract and Payment

    Total hours:

    Total contract:

    Contract signed:

    Total charges:

    Deposit amount:

        Due:

            Payment: Credit card

                         Check (check #:   )

    Final Payment amount:

        Due:

            Payment: Credit card

                         Check (check #:   )

Montage

A montage is a short video of memories usually 7- 9 minutes long shown during a slow period or looping during the cocktail hour on a screen large enough for all to see.

- Add music to the montage to keep it entertaining.

- Bring two copies to the event.

- Have the kids sit on the dance floor – it is easier to control them.

- Pay a professional to play the montage.

- Hook the sound to a monitor or the musical entertainment so everyone can hear

- Try to include all guests or only family.

- Test your montage on sight or with the actual equipment that it will be shown with.

Creating and Organizing Your Montage

Things to consider when collecting photos and videos:
- Approximately 100 photos and 5 video clips (equals video length of 6 – 8 in minutes)
- Sort photos into about 4-5 folders/categories
  - Activities
  - Baby
  - Family
  - Friends
  - Honoree, solo pictures
  - Siblings
  - One may happen organically (ex. photos of halloween/child falling asleep/sports, hair or eyes, etc.)

Types of photos to select:
- Honoree participating in a variety of activities
  - Field trips
  - Hobbies: Sports, musical activities
  - Holidays/birthdays
  - Vacations
  - Volunteering/Clubs
- Honoree should be included in all photos
- Mixture of family and friend photos

Types of videos to select:
- Ages 6 – 18 months
  - Cute expressions
  - Giggling
  - Milestones: first step, first word
- Ages 2 – 7 years
  - Milestones: first day of school, bike riding, sport teams, performances, recitals
- Ages 8 – 13 Years
  - Milestones: performances, recitals, sports achievements

Find a Pattern:
- Milestones
- Recurring event - one photo from every year depicting the following events:
  - First day of school
  - Halloween costumes

- - Special experience – visited all 50 states
  - Yearly birthday celebrations
  - Yearly vacation
- Through the years (photos in chronological order)

Categorize your photos and videos to be compiled into the montage

Choose your music
- Fun to listen to
- Memorable
- Personal
- Popular
- Specific to family or an event

Decide how this montage is going to be shown at your event
- On the rented screens (typically through your MC) - LED players
- With your laptop on a pull up screen or screens provided by the venue
  - consider if the sound needs to be played through the MC speakers

Get it tested ahead of time always

Montage Information Sheet

Basic Information

    Company:

    Contact person:

    Phone:

    E-mail:

    Cell:

    Fax:

    Address:

Contract and Payment

    Total hours:

    Total contract:

    Contract signed:

    Total charges:

    Deposit amount:

        Due:

            Payment: Credit card

                            Check (check #:   )

    Final Payment amount:

        Due:

            Payment: Credit card

                            Check (check #:   )

SECTION 9: DÉCOR

Flowers and décor are the most creative and unique parts of your event.

- Are there volunteer flower or decoration arrangers on site? Check with your florist before you commit volunteer help.

- Can ceremony flowers or decorations be used later for the reception? Who will be responsible for moving and rearranging them?

- Decide what to do with the flowers or decorations post-event, you may want to keep several items as keepsakes, donate them to the local retirement home, or distribute them to guests.

- Is there another event at the venue the same day? Can any flowers or decorations be shared? How will this affect set-up and turnover time?

- Leave specific instructions about where and how to set up flower arrangements or decorations for anyone who will be helping with set-up and arrangements.

- Logos play a big part in décor in today's celebrations

- Make sure your centerpieces do not block conversations

- Make sure your centerpieces allow for table space especially if you are serving family style

- When can the flowers or decorations arrive and who will be delivering them?

- When can the flowers or decorations be set up and who will be arranging them on site?

- When must rentals like vases and centerpieces be returned or picked up?

Décor consists of the following items

- Balloons
- candles
- centerpieces
- chairs
- chair with arms for hora
- cocktail hour decor
- entrance arches
- entertainment
- envelope box
- flat screens
- facades
- furniture
- lighting
- linens
- logos
- napkins
- pipe and drape
- place cards
- place card table centerpiece
- room decor
- sign in item
- signage
- sign in item
- tables
- votives

Flowers and Décor Information Sheet

Basic Information

    Company:

    Contact person:

    Phone:

    E-mail:

    Cell:

    Fax:

    Address:

Contract and Payment

    Total hours:

    Total contract:

    Contract signed:

    Total charges:

    Deposit amount:

        Due:

        Payment: Credit card

                       Check (check #:   )

    Final Payment amount:

        Due:

        Payment: Credit card

                       Check (check #:   )

Themes

Many people choose to plan their event based on a particular theme like ...

- a carnival
- a city (Los Angeles, Miami, New York, etc.)
- a club
- a season ("Winter Wonderland," etc.)
- a television show or movie (cartoons, The Hunger Games, etc.)
- an awards ceremony or red carpet (Emmy, Grammy, Oscar, Tony, etc.)
- candy
- colors or a specific color
- flowers or a specific flower
- music (a band or singer, a genre, a song, a concert, etc.)
- sports or a specific sport (players, teams, etc.)
- stars and celebrities
- theatre (Broadway, a Broadway show, Musical Theatre, etc.)

A theme ties together your party's segments like decorations and entertainment. A logo or slogan helps, for example:

- I danced all night with ...
- I went around the world with ...
- _____'s Caribbean Paradise
- I tangoed at the mango
- _____'s Red Carpet Night
- _____'s Stadium
- Club _____
- _____ Night Live

Balloons/Decorations Information Sheet

Basic Information

    Company:

    Contact person:

    Phone:

    E-mail:

    Cell:

    Fax:

    Address:

Contract and Payment

    Total hours:

    Total contract:

    Contract signed:

    Total charges:

    Deposit amount:

        Due:

        Payment: Credit card

                          Check (check #:   )

    Final Payment amount:

        Due:

        Payment: Credit card

                          Check (check #:   )

                                Additional Décor

Lighting

Lighting is additional décor that can have a huge impact ant it may not even require a line item on the budget. Review the lighting at your venue -- is it adjustable? Is it too much or too little? Is there outside lighting if you need it?

Simple, cost effective lighting includes:

- Ambiance is lighting that lowers the lighting for elegance.
- Candles with fire or batteries provide ambiance.
- Centerpiece lighting is used to highlight your table and décor.
- Chachkies are giveaway items typically provided by your DJ/Band. They usually will offer plenty of items that light up, blow up and make noise to hand out all night long.
- Dance floor lighting is usually provided by your musicians. Gobo is the "go between" or "goes before optics" that creates a design or pattern out of the light to flash a logo on the floor or wall.
- Pin lighting is a narrow beam of light used to showcase a special feature like a cake.
- Specialty lighting is for your ice carving, a water feature, or to focus everyone on a ceremony or speaker.
- Up-lighting is a beam of light in any color washed up on the walls, pillars or trees.

Lighting Information Sheet

Basic Information

    Company:

    Contact person:

    Phone:

    E-mail:

    Cell:

    Fax:

    Address:

Contract and Payment

    Total hours:

    Total contract:

    Contract signed:

    Total charges:

    Deposit amount:

        Due:

        Payment: Credit card

                          Check (check #:   )

    Final Payment amount:

        Due:

        Payment: Credit card

                          Check (check #:   )

SECTION 10: RENTALS AND FAVORS

Almost any décor or decoration can be rented, including ...

- Bars
- Chairs and chair covers
- Dance floors
- Dishes and flatware
- Entertainment (games, photo booths, etc.)
- Food and drink machines (frozen yogurt machines, cotton candy machines, smoothie machines, etc.)
- Furniture (couches, chairs, etc.)
- Heating or air-conditioning
- Lighting
- Pipe and drape
- Special décor and decorative items (fog machines, disco balls, balloons, backdrops, etc.)
- Tables and linens (see guests seating section)
- Tableware, silverware, and glassware
- Tents (for outdoor events)

Other items can be purchased including ...

- Candles
- Centerpieces
- Cocktail napkins
- Furniture (inflatable furniture, bean bag furniture, etc.)
- Special décor and decorative items (neon or lighted signs, ice sculptures, balloon designs, etc.)
- Special drink glasses (glowing or lighted glasses, decorated glass, etc.)

> **NOTE**: Ask for more information about SAVE *The* DATE, LLC EVENTS "day-of" service, which takes care of all of the above and more.

Rentals Information Sheet

Basic Information

    Company:

    Contact person:

    Phone:

    E-mail:

    Cell:

    Fax:

    Address:

Contract and Payment

    Total hours:

    Total contract:

    Contract signed:

    Total charges:

    Deposit amount:

        Due:

            Payment: Credit card

                          Check (check #:   )

    Final Payment amount:

        Due:

            Payment: Credit card

                          Check (check #:   )

Linen Rentals Information Sheet

Basic Information

    Company:

    Contact person:

    Phone:

    E-mail:

    Cell:

    Fax:

    Address:

Contract and Payment

    Total hours:

    Total contract:

    Contract signed:

    Total charges:

    Deposit amount:

        Due:

        Payment: Credit card

                        Check (check #:   )

    Final Payment amount:

        Due:

        Payment: Credit card

                        Check (check #:   )

Parking/Transportation

Details matter, so if you as host need to cut the budget to pay for parking, it is wise to make sure your guests never open their wallet. Your event planner or venue manager can guide you to the best method for parking, which may be a ticket given out at the bar, mailed prior to the event, or a list kept at the valet stand.

Just remember to ask!

- Bus Options

  - Consider a bus or other type of transportation to get your guests from place to place, especially for unaccompanied minors going from the temple to a party.

  - Have an older teen or adult chaperone on the bus

  - Mail out information concerning any offered transportation and get rsvp's

  - Prepare a complete list of children's names for who will take the bus

  - Put a sign on the bus outside of the Synagogue designating which is the bus for your event and have the Rabbi announce the instructions at the end of the service

- Valet Options

  - Consider having a sign including that the "tip" has been provided by your host to keep your wallets closed.

  - Let your guests know you are offering valet.

  - Remember to have more staff available at the start of your event for overflow.

  - Think about having the bus drop off the kids at a different entrance.

Valet Information Sheet

Basic Information

    Company:

    Contact person:

    Phone:

    E-mail:

    Cell:

    Fax:

    Address:

Contract and Payment

    Total hours:

    Total contract:

    Contract signed:

    Total charges:

    Deposit amount:

        Due:

        Payment: Credit card

                        Check (check #:   )

    Final Payment amount:

        Due:

        Payment: Credit card

                        Check (check #:   )

Transportation Information Sheet

Basic Information

    Company:

    Contact person:

    Phone:

    E-mail:

    Cell:

    Fax:

    Address:

Contract and Payment

    Total hours:

    Total contract:

    Contract signed:

    Total charges:

    Deposit amount:

        Due:

        Payment: Credit card

                          Check (check #:   )

    Final Payment amount:

        Due:

        Payment: Credit card

                          Check (check #:   )

Security

Providing security at your teen's event is no longer as an option. It is not only for the safety of your guests but more often for controlling teenage guests. Today's teens need to be "watched" more than ever!

Use the following as a starting place for determining how much security is needed:

- Cell phone use?
- Do the children dance or are they harder to please?
- How many children will attend?
- Is this a Bat (girls) or Bar (boys) Mitzvah?
- Where is your event? How spread out is it?
- What is required in the venue's contract?
- How old are the kids (young 13 or older 13)?
- What is the dress code of the event?

The general rule is to have 1 security guard for every 45 minors. Make sure you are hiring security that knows what they are there for, meaning they have worked Mitzvahs before.

- The security guard can dress in a suit or professional manner or in a fun "bouncer" shirt.
- 1 guard should stay "around" the kid's area and 1 should stay in the hallway near the doors.
- Remember to feed security as though they are vendors also.

Keep this in mind. Your synagogue sometimes offers security or requires that you pay for security, this is not the same security. This is security keeping watch of the synagogue itself and keeping your guests safe from the outside, not keeping the synagogue safe from the kids.

Security Information Sheet

Basic Information

    Company:

    Contact person:

    Phone:

    E-mail:

    Cell:

    Fax:

    Address:

Contract and Payment

    Total hours:

    Total contract:

    Contract signed:

    Total charges:

    Deposit amount:

        Due:

            Payment: Credit card

                          Check (check #:   )

    Final Payment amount:

        Due:

            Payment: Credit card

                          Check (check #:   )

SECTION 11: FAVORS AND BRANDING

Favors are generally for the kids. Your child will have insight into what he/she wants and what his/her crowd will appreciate.

- Questions to ask:
    - Can this favor have more than one use at the party? Some favors can be place cards, chair/table décor, or entertainment.
    - Do you want to include adults in receiving favors?
    - Do you have a "logo" to use on the favor?
    - Do you need different sizes or colors – female/male?
    - How much can you afford to spend per child? per couple?
    - Is it a favor worthy of keeping? Or is it junk?
    - What does your child have in mind?

- Specific to your event
    - Does the favor match the theme?
    - Is the favor memorable?
    - Is the favor appropriate to the times?
    - When do you want to distribute the favor?

An advertising specialty professional can help with gifts, especially if you would like a logo, but typical favors include:

- Bags
- Blankets
- Candy
- Cell phone accessories
- Clothing (*young people put new clothes immediately, so the clothes they arrived in will not be in the photos. Consider giving clothing out late in your party*)
- Donation certificates
- Electronic accessories
- Hats
- Jewelry
- Light up fans
- Mugs
- Pens
- Personalized pads
- Socks
- Themed cups
- Water bottles   Much, much more …

Favors Information Sheet

Basic Information

    Company:

    Contact person:

    Phone:

    E-mail:

    Cell:

    Fax:

    Address:

Contract and Payment

    Total hours:

    Total contract:

    Contract signed:

    Total charges:

    Deposit amount:

        Due:

            Payment: Credit card

                            Check (check #:   )

    Final Payment amount:

        Due:

            Payment: Credit card

                            Check (check #:   )

Branding your party with a logo

- A logo helps to "define" your event.
- You can incorporate your décor around your logo.
- Your logo will generally be designed by an artist and will need to be provided in several formats for using at your event (pdf, jpg, eps or others).
- Be sure to get your logo to all of your vendors so they use it at your event.
- Places vendors will incorporate your logo are:
    - cocktail napkins
    - flat screens
    - invitation
    - menu
    - montage
    - photo favor
- How you can get started on a logo design?
    - Do some internet research by looking up logos for inspiration. Follow all copyright laws.
    - Examples of logos are:

   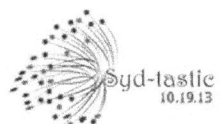  

- This is a sample of "logo" creation steps:

- What does a logo include?
  - a theme, interest or design
  - date of event
  - honorees first, middle and last name or initials
  - specific colors
- examples of font styles:

ALGERIAN   AR Delaney   Broadway   Kristin ITC

Kunstler Script   Lucida Calligraphy   Magneto

Onyx   Ravie   STENCIL

Other Items

You may wish to personalize other items, for example:

- bags to hold the giveaways
- baskets for kippot, socks, or favors
- bathroom décor
- candle lighting items
- candy
- chachkies (given out on the dance floor)
- cocktail napkins (3-4 per person)
- decorative extras
- envelope basket with a lock
- flat screens
- guest bathroom towels (2 per person)
- invitation or other printed materials
- kippot
- light up paraphernalia
- menus
- mitzvah project items
- photo booth pictures or other entertainment items
- place cards
- prizes
- signage
- socks for the girls
- table card names
- tallis

Other Retail Information Sheet

Basic Information

    Company:

    Contact person:

    Phone:

    E-mail:

    Cell:

    Fax:

    Address:

A list and description of the item(s):

Total:

    Deposit amount:

        Due:

        Payment: Credit card

                      Check (check #:   )

    Final Payment amount:

        Due:

        Payment: Credit card

                      Check (check #:   )

SECTION 12: INVITATIONS

Begin looking at invitations and/or "save the date" announcements 5-6 months before your event and order two months before the mailing date.

Order at least twenty-five (25) extra ceremony and/or reception invitations, thank-you cards, and envelopes for last minute invites, returned addresses and the like. This will cost less than placing a new order later.

In addition to the above extras, order at least twenty-five (25) additional envelopes *in case of mistakes or printing errors.*

Decide if you want a professional calligrapher to address your envelopes:
- The calligrapher can help you decide if you want handwritten or machine calligraphy with what font and color.

- Provide your calligrapher with a typed list of guests' names and addresses in the exact format you would like them to appear -- Bob and Edna Smith, Mr. and Mrs. Bob Smith, Mr. and Mrs. Bob Smith, etc.

- If your calligrapher will be stuffing, stamping, and mailing your invitations, be sure to provide all the inserts, instructions and stamps.

Helpful tips for ordering your invitations ...
- Take a sample invitation and sample response card to the post office to verify the postage on each.

- Creating your own stamps is a nice touch. You can do this all on the **SAVE** *The* **DATE** web site with just a few clicks. Remember to make stamps for your response cards as well.

  - Send the invitations for local invitees 8-10 weeks before the event; for out-of-town invitees, 10--12 weeks ahead of time.

  - Families plan their holidays well in advance, so send your invitations for a holiday event at least 10-12 weeks ahead of time.

- Hand-cancel your invitations at the post office to prevent the haphazard machine cancel. Your guests will receive a prettier overall invitation.

- Consider self-stick envelopes.

- Consider having it compliment your "save the date".

- Send out "save the dates" up to 6 months in advance

    - "save the date" should go to everyone

    - You can always add people to your list after a "save the date" goes out, you can't take a "save the date" back

Invitation Information Sheet

Basic Information

    Company:

    Contact person:

    Phone:

    E-mail:

    Cell:

    Fax:

    Address:

Total Save-the-date Invitations:
Total Ceremony Invitations:
Total Ceremony Invitations Envelopes:
Total Reception Invitations:
Total Reception Invitations Envelopes:
Total Response Cards:
Total Response Cards Envelopes:
Total Thank You Notes:
Total Thank You Notes Envelopes:
Total Stamps:

Contract and Payment

    Total hours:

    Total contract:

    Contract signed:

    Total charges:

    Deposit amount:

        Due:

        Payment: Credit card

                           Check (check #:   )

    Final Payment amount:

        Due:

        Payment: Credit card

                           Check (check #:   )

Items Needed for Invitations

Company: _____ Book: _____ Page #: _____

Quantity	Price per 100	Additional 25's

_____ invitation _____ _____

_____ invitation return address _____ _____

_____ invitation envelope liners _____ _____

_____ reception cards _____ _____

_____ response cards _____ _____

_____ response return address _____ _____

_____ thank you/informal _____ _____

_____ thank you return address _____ _____

Add on items:

_____ additional layers/paper/die cut _____ _____

_____ camera ready art _____ _____

_____ custom font _____ _____

_____ direction card _____ _____

_____ ink color _____ _____

_____ language change _____ _____

_____ mailer seal _____ _____

_____ place cards _____ _____

_____ self-sealing envelopes _____ _____

Additional charges include tax, proofs, shipping and handling.

© SAVE *The* DATE, LLC EVENTS

events and promotions your way
WWW.SaveTheDateLLCEvents.com

Sample Invitation

Invitation

Please join us as our son
Tommy Rock
(Hebrew)
is called to the Torah as a Bar Mitzvah
Saturday, the eleventh of November, two thousand and fourteen
At nine-thirty in the morning
location
City, State

The celebration continues with dinner and dancing
At seven-thirty in the evening
location
City, State

Nancy and Jim Rock

Return address invitation

1515 Rock Drive
North Potomac, Maryland 20878

Response card

Please reply before October 21

Name/s _____
_____will attend
_____will not attend

Number attending _____

Front return address response

Nancy and Jim Rock
1515 Rock Drive
North Potomac, Maryland 20878

Thank you

Tommy Rock

Return address thank you

1515 Rock Drive
North Potomac, Maryland 20878

© SAVE The DATE, LLC EVENTS
events and promotions your way
WWW.SaveTheDateLLCEvents.com

Sample Invitation Phrases

Special moments in our lives
are meant to be shared with family and friends

…

Please join us in celebrating the Bar/Bat Mitzvah of

…

Please join us as our son
John Matthew
is called to the Torah as a Bar Mitzvah

…

It is with great pride and joy
that we invite you to join us

…

request the pleasure of your company
at the Bar Mitzvah of their son

…

Please share in our happiness
when our daughter
Rachel
will be called to the Torah
as a Bat Mitzvah

…

With pride and joy we invite you to share
a special day in our lives

…

Mr. and Mrs. John Doe
cordially invite you to join them
at the Bat Mitzvah of their daughter

…

At this very special time in our lives we invite our
family and friends to worship with us when our son

…

In the tradition of our fathers and fathers before him

…

On this very special day
We invite our family and friends

…

Special occasions become treasured memories (special moments)
when shared with family and friends

…

With love in our hearts we invite you, our friends and family,
to join us for the

© SAVE The DATE, LLC EVENTS
events and promotions your way
WWW.SaveTheDateLLCEvents.com

...
In honor of a beautiful tradition
We invite you to share our joy

...
Together with my family we invite you
to share the occasion of my Bat Mitzvah

...
Memories are created by sharing special moments
with family and friends

...
Our hearts will be filled with love when those
who are close and dear to us share this special moment

...
We would be delighted to have you
join us when our daughter

...
With pride, joy and lots of love
we invite you to share this special day

...
Special moments become
beautiful memories when shared with family and friends

...
Please share this moment with us

...
To fulfill her/his commitment to Judaism

...
Our world reflects a rich tradition of yesterday and the bright promise of
tomorrow as our son is called to read from the Torah

...
We welcome you to share our joy

...
Life's special moments are even more joyous when shared
with friends and family

...
Please share this cherished moment

Sample Invitation Response Cards

We look forward to seeing you.
Please respond by May 4
M_____
_____will attend
_____will not attend

...

The favor of a reply is requested before
May 4, 2018
Name/s _____
will _____ attend

...

The favor of a reply is requested by May 4, 2018
M_____
_____ persons will attend
Please initial entrée selection:
____ Norwegian Salmon ____ Chicken Marsala ____ Prime Rib

...

Looking forward to celebrating with you!
Please respond by the Fourth of May

...

Kindly (or please) respond by

...

Just Say Yes, and say it by May 4th

...

Your presence will be very special to us

...

Your early reply will be appreciated

...

will attend / will not attend

...

accepts with pleasure / declines with regret

...

can't wait to party/party on without us

...

love to/broken hearted

...

love to attend / crushed to miss it

...

wouldn't miss it / celebrating from afar

© SAVE The DATE, LLC EVENTS
events and promotions your way
WWW.SaveTheDateLLCEvents.com

Hebrew Phrases

If you want your child's Hebrew name in the invitation, ask your Rabbi/Cantor to write out the Hebrew version and the English transliterations of your child's name with the letters in the correct (right to left) backwards order.

Bar Mitzvah (בר מצוה)- boy's Mitzvah

Bat Mitzvah (בת מצוה)– girl's Mitzvah

A Hebrew phrase is sometimes put on the invitations as a sign of thoughtfulness or the utmost care. Almost like a general symbol placed in a letter. Think of it as an emoji symbol telling others how you feel. Again, written right to left

The most popular location for a Hebrew phrase is in the right top corner copy, and the most popular phrases are:

Bais Hey (ב"ה)– blessed is G-d – We want good things to happen to the person

Bet Samech Daled (בס"ד)– with help from God

B'Ezrat Hashem (בעזרת ה') – the long version of above with god's help abbreviated version is Bes Hey (above)

B'Simcha Rabah (בשמחה רבה) - with much joy

If you are writing a card to the B'nai Mitzvah
Mazel Tov (מזל טוב) – congratulations

If the simcha is during the high holidays
Shanah Tovah (שנה טובה) – happy new year – sweet new year

For use on thank you notes -
Todah (תודה) – thank you

Some companies require forms which you must fil out in order to get the Hebrew added.

Be sure to check your proof carefully several times!

Now Draft Your Own Invitation!

Front return address response

Invitation

Reception card

Response card

Return address invitation

Return address thank you

Thank you

Optional:

Direction card

Friday night/after-party card(s)

Teen card

Transportation card

SECTION 13: OTHER PRINTING

Emails may serve as communications to replace traditional communications, but depending the formality of your event, be prepared to print:

A **friends and family letters/shabbat dinner/out-of-towners letter** with invitations to additional events and hotel information like special prearranged group rates, *phone numbers, locations, reservation information, and mileage from the event location(s) and from major transportation.*

A **kid's/parent's letter** sent 1-2 weeks before the event to remind kids of the upcoming event and to tell parents about:
- transportation from the ceremony to the reception (*if necessary*)
- emergency contact information *(names and cell phone numbers)*
- appropriate dress for the services and the party
- appropriate behavior
- pick-up times and instructions. It is a good idea to ask that parents come into the party to pick up their children, rather than let the children leave the party unsupervised.

The **program**, if the temple allows it. Information may be requested for the general program such as who will be reciting prayers, making an aliyah or speeches, etc.

Tags are for labeling favors, especially if sizes are specified or the item is not to be confused with other's belongings.

Place cards for seating arrangements and meal choice with or without **escort cards** used to let which guests know their table name or number.

If you choose to have your own design instead of the caterer's, **cocktail napkins** (with printing or your logo) can be used for drinks and hors' d'oeuvres. The rule of thumb is 4 per person.

Bathroom hand towels (with printing or logo) at 2-3 per person.

Other Printing Information Sheet

Basic Information

    Company:

    Contact person:

    Phone:

    E-mail:

    Cell:

    Fax:

    Address:

Information Totals:
    bathroom hand towels (with logo):
    brunch letters:
    cocktail napkins (with logo):
    Other letters: friends and family letters, out-of-town letters, parents letter
    place cards:
    programs:

Contract and Payment Information
    Contract signed:
    Total charges:

Contract and Payment

    Contract signed:

    Total charges:

    Deposit amount:

        Due:

        Payment: credit card

                        check (check #:   )

    Final payment amount:

        Due:

        Payment: credit card

                        check (check #:   )

© SAVE The DATE, LLC EVENTS
events and promotions your way
WWW.SaveTheDateLLCEvents.com

Out of Town Guest Letter

Your out-of-town guests will appreciate being together and receiving information that makes their trip easier. Begin looking for hotel accommodations 6 to 7 months before your event and consider:

- Consider reserving a block of rooms, which you may have to do to receive a discounted rate. Ask for the rooms can be located near each other, the same floor for example). Ask about room-block policies.

- amenities like restaurants, room service, exercise rooms, pools, salons, etc.

- the location and convenience of the hotel(s) including access to car rentals, metro stations, buses, etc.

- safety: even the best rates and amenities don't trump an unsafe hotel or area.

If possible, offer two hotel options at different prices. When you have chosen the hotel(s), ask the hotel(s) about offering discounted rates in a room block and whether your block's rooms can be near each other.

Then provide your guests with a reservation card with your invitations. The card should include the hotel's name, phone number, and information about booking rooms at the discounted rate. A list of suggestions for restaurants, attractions, shops, or other places they may enjoy visiting helps out-of-town guests with planning.

An optional item that you can choose to skip, but guests enjoy receiving a little something upon their arrival, so consider providing a welcome note and gift basket that you deliver to your hotel with names of guests on a tag for the hotel front desk associate to hand to the appropriate guest or leave in their room.

The gift basket should include the welcome letter, but past that think of local or unique items that may have meaning to you, like Boston baked beans if you are from Boston, or a selection of drinks, snacks, or toys.

Provide one main welcome item – ex. large cookie, box of cookies, chocolate covered pretzels, etc.

> **TIP**: Generally, hotel desk will hand these to your guests as they arrive at no charge; however, most will charge to deliver your welcome item(s) to the guest rooms.

Welcome Basket Information Sheet

Basic Information

    Company:

    Contact person:

    Phone:

    E-mail:

    Cell:

    Fax:

    Address:

Purchase Totals
    baskets:
    drinks:
    snacks:
    toys:
    other:
        Total:

Contract and Payment

    Total hours:

    Total contract:

    Contract signed:

    Total charges:

    Deposit Amount:
        Due:
        Payment: Credit card
                          Check (check #:   )

    Final Payment Amount:
        Due:
        Payment: Credit card
                          Check (check #:   )

© SAVE The DATE, LLC EVENTS
events and promotions your way
WWW.SaveTheDateLLCEvents.com

Sample Welcome Letter

WELCOME TO _____'S CELEBRATION WEEKEND!
We are so excited to have you join us on this very special weekend! Please enjoy the snack and drinks we made especially for you.
Take home the _____
as our gift to you to remember your time here.
We look forward to seeing you
Friday night at our home,
Saturday morning at the Temple,
and at _____
in the evening for the big celebration!
Finally, don't forget to join us Sunday morning for our farewell brunch.

Love, From_____

Sample Friends and Family Letter

Dear Family and Friends,

We are looking forward to having you join us for _____'s big weekend! It promises to be a wonderful time filled with excitement. We have gathered information for you that we know will be helpful.

We have set aside rooms from _____until _____and arranged for special rates at the hotel where our celebration will be. It is approximately 5 miles to the Temple services by ___ (car only, bus, we have arranged). The rates are $____for a standard room, ____ for a deluxe room and _____for a suite. Breakfast is included with your reservation. It is our pleasure to have a hosted hospitality room available for all our guests all weekend where you are welcome to kick up your feet and relax outside of your hotel room. Please call _____and request room block code _____before_____. The hotel is very lovely and in the heart of _____ with_____ amenities. A shuttle is available for local transportation with the Washington D.C. Metro rail system just a 10 minute drive away.

For the schedule of festivities:

_____: Shabbat Services and Sabbath dinner at _____.
Please join us for Services to begin at 7:00 pm followed by an informal Sabbath dinner at _____in _____, Maryland.

_____: The Big B'nai Mitzvah Day! Services at _____begin promptly at __:__ in the morning followed by a celebration oneg meal. Relax in the afternoon, so you'll be ready to celebrate and dance the night away at the Bar Mitzvah celebration that begins promptly at 7:30. We hope you can stay all night with us because we are planning an exciting night with many fun surprises including breakfast to be served at 1:00 am.

© SAVE *The* DATE, LLC EVENTS
events and promotions your way
WWW.SaveTheDateLLCEvents.com

_____Please join us for breakfast from _____ at _____.

Allow from the hotel to:
- Reagan National Airport – 30 minute drive south
- Dulles Airport – 40 minute drive southwest
- Baltimore Washington Airport – 40 minute drive north
- Union Station – 35 minute drive south

We can't wait to see you!

Sample Parent/Children Letter

Dear Parents,

We are delighted that your child will be joining us when _____ becomes a Ba_____ Mitzvah and reads from the Torah for the first time. Please find a few important details for the service and celebration:

Shabbat Morning at _____
Services will begin at _____. The Torah service should start around ____. Due to the religious component, appropriate dress is as follows: sports jacket or suit and tie for the boys, and dressy clothing with covered shoulders for the girls.

_____ is a conservative synagogue. Please have your children turn-off their cell phones before arriving at the synagogue, or plan to leave them at home. If your child must use her/his phone, please remind them to do so outside the building and to keep the phones put away while in the service. The use of any electronics (including cellphones) is not permitted in the building on Shabbat.

The service will end around _____ and will be followed by a Kiddush lunch. The menu includes kosher deli and other vegetarian options. Please let us know if your child has any dietary issues that you need to discuss. If you are trying to schedule a pickup time, people typically begin to disperse around ____.

Saturday evening party at _____
The evening will begin at ____ and consist of dinner, dancing, and other entertainment. The dress is _____ attire.

We will be serving kosher meat and other vegetarian options. Again please let us know if you have any dietary concerns that you would like us to be aware of.

We will not be gathering cellphones, but encourage the children to either leave their phones at home or to refrain from using them other than for taking pictures at the party. We have cubbies that they can put their phones into.

The Last dance will be at ____. We ask that you come inside to pick-up your children or have them check-in with ____ before they leave.

If you have any questions, please call our party planner _____ from **SAVE** *The* **DATE**, LLC at _____. Thank you and we look forward to having your child attend this special day.

Thank you for helping us celebrate!

The Program

The program includes information about the service and who is participating. Personalized or the general temple programs with personalization can include photos, personal statements, speeches, and more. Temple programs are general and shorter.

Programs are given out at the service along with Kippot and include:

- Hebrew date, name, and Hebrew name
- Mitzvah projects
- Brief education on the history and symbolic meaning of the service
- Recognition of relatives who have died
- Location of portions
- Explanations of what Torah and/or Haftarah portion is about

If your temple prints your program, you are generally asked a few basic questions that they will add into the layout for you.

If you are making your own program there are experienced companies that can do this for you, or you can do it yourself.

Sample Program

The Villa
Shabbat Afternoon Service

November 20, 2010
6 Adar 5770

logo

BAT MITZVAH OF

Morgan Machado

Torah Porton:
Plaut Torah Book: -
pages
Ezekial Tetzavah 43:10-17
pages

Rabbi

We recognize and honor the following special people for participating in today's service...

Honor	Honoree
Presenting the Tallit	Jerry and Sandy Weisberg Marci's Maternal Grandfather and Grandma Sandy
Reading	Jay and Linda Weiss Marci's Paternal Grandparents
Undressing the Torah	Zachary Weiss Marci's Brother
Torah Aliyah #1	Michael and Rebecca Weiss Larry and Barbra Weisberg Rachel and Scott Carr
Torah Aliyah #2	Marci's Aunts and Uncles
Bat Mitzvah Aliyah	Joel and Cara Weiss Marci's Parents
Dressing The Torah	Marci Leah Weiss
	Risa and Danny Korn

During the service, people may need to walk in or out of the Sanctuary when the ark is open, the congregation is standing, the Rabbi is giving the sermon, or when other persons are addressing the Congregation from the pulpit. Applause is not appropriate during the service and photography is not permitted.

Please remember to turn of all cell phones and electronic devices.
If you need any assistance, please ask an usher, who will be hapy to help make your worship experience at Temple Beth Ami a meaninbgful and enjoyable one.
Hearing devices and large print prayerbooks are available.
Shabbat Shalom

Welcome

Dearest family, friends and members of our Congregation,

    We thank you for joining us for Marci's Bat Mitzvah and sharing this joyous occasion with us!
Cherished moments become memories when surrounding by those we love.

                       Cara, Joel Marci and Zach

Torah Portion

Tetzevah

When God taught the wandering Jews the steps they should take to develop Jewish souls

Haftorah Portion

Parke Avot

Jewish Ethics project:

Mitzvah Project

Birthday Dreams Come True
Every child dreams of a Birthday party. Marci and 4 close friends from Temple Beth Ami have built a web site and a program (Birthdaywishes.org.) Providing monthly birthday parties for children who reside temporarily at "The Stepping Stones Shelter".

Havdallah

Please join us in the main entrance of our Temple to celebrate havdallah where we will surround the memorial wall and close our service with memories of Marci's late grandmother Myrna, recognizing her plaque on our Temple wall. Join us as we remember and pray.

Havdallah

To seperate yourself from the unholy: strive for holidness. Havdallah is derived from the hebrew word meaning "to divide". It usually takes place at the conclusion of the Sabbath or Festival, dividing the special or holy day from the ordinary weekdays. As the sabbath is ushered in with candlelight and a blessing over thh wine, so too is its departure accompanied by candlelight, wine and prayer. We also inhale the fragrent spices contained in the Besamim Box symbolizing our hope that the coming week will be sweet and pleasant.

Service

Save us, O Lord, answer us, O king, when we call upon You. Give us lights and joy, gladness and honor, as in the happiest days of Israel's past. Then we will lift up the cup to rejoice in Your saving power, and call out Your name in praise.
                The Wine, The spice box, The braided candle.

> This Havdallah service is in honor and memory of those whoe love caring, commitment and sacrifice provided the foundation for who we are today.

6,000,000 Jews who perished in the Holocaust
we shall never forget
Myrna Weisberg
Minnie & Moe Jacobs, Frances & Louis Adler, Mildred & Joseph Weiss
beloved Jersey - our best friend.

Barchu

Barchu is the call to worship inviting the entire congregation to pray. *Shema* (Deut 6.4) is the ceteral prayer of the Jewish faith. We declare our belief in one God, who is the God of all people. The *Shema* (Hear O Israel, the Lord is our God, the Lord is One) is the first prayer that a Jewish child is taught and the last a person says on the approach of death *V'ahavta* (Deut. 6:5-9) instructs us to loe God and keep the commandents (mitzvot).

Amidah

Amidah which means "standing", is the core of the prayer service. It is a collection of belssings. Avot v'imahot invokes the names of our biblical mothers and fathers and praises God; Kadosh describes the holiness of God. We conclude with a prayer for peace.

Aleinu

This part of the service, sung before the open ark, is also known as the "adoration". It expresses praise and adoration of God as the infinite Creator and Ruler. The text affirms the hope for a time when all will acknowledge God's being, sovereignty, and requirements and we will live without war, malice, hatred, or oppression.

Mourner's Kaddish

A "kaddish" is recited to signal the conclusion of a section of prayer. There are four forms of Kaddish throughout our service, one of which (Mourner's) is the prayer for those in mourning or for those remembering the anniversary of the passing of a loved one. In some congregations only mourners rise to recite this prayer. At Temple Beth Ami, all present rise while Kaddish is recited.

Ark

The focal point of our sanctuary. It houses the Torah scrolls and is customarily located on an eastern wall to help orient the congregation towards jerusalem. Above the Ark is an Eternal Light, which burns continuously as a sign of God's presence.

* Traditions

BAT MITZVAH

The word "Bat" is Hebrew for daughter. A "Mitzvah" is a commandment. A Jewish daughter is obligated to observe the commandments and traditions of Judiasm.

Today's ceremony marks a passage into adult status in the Jewish community. The Bat Mitzvah commits herself to a lifetime of study of the ideals of Torah, and is expected to assume moral responsibility for her actions and to contribute to the welfare of the community.

TORAH SERVICE

The reading of the Torah is the highlight of the service for the Bat Mitzvah. The Torah contains the first five books of the Bible, the oldest section written over 3000 years ago. to read from the scroll is both an honor and privilege and no act symbolizes becoming a Bat Mitzvah more than this reading.

The Torah is divided into 54 parts which in the course of an Jewish Calendar year, part of every portion of the entire Torah is read. Each week throughout the world, the same portion of the Torah is chanted in synagogues and congregations all over the world , along with a corresponding passage from the Prophets, called the Haftorah.

HAFTORAH SERVICE

The reading of the haftorah is the corresponding passage from the Troah which was from the Prophets

Tallit/Kipah/Tzit Tzit

Jewish tradition encourages worshippers to cover their heads during prayer service with a kipah as a sign of respect for God. Tallit (four cornered prayer shawl) is worn by Jews over the age of Bar or Bat Mitzvah in fulfillment of the biblical commandment to wear tzit tzit or fringes on the corners of all four-cornered garments, as a reminder of God's commandments. Typically worn by only men and boys, in more liberal synagogues like ours, both men and women may chose to wear them.

* Excerpts from other Temples and Synnagogues have been borrowed to assist us in developing this program.

Place Cards

"Place card" and "escort card" are used interchangeably but they are different. The place card is at a person's assigned seat and indicates their meal choice. The escort card is traditionally on the place card table and indicates the table where a couple is to be seated.

Place cards and card holders can be formal or imaginative:

- a paper card in mini envelopes or on themed ceramic holders

- a tent cards with or without an appliqué design

- a place cardboard, a poster or blackboard on an easel with guest's names in alphabetical order or by table

- theme cards written on or attached to a paper card -- bottled water, candy, carabineers, glow balls, hotel key cards, key chains, leaves, lollipops, noisemakers, picture frames, sunglasses or whatever you find in keeping with your theme.

For a different feel, not everyone assigns seats although one may find that not everyone finds a seat (like a group of four who wanted to sit together). Some guests may feel lost and try to "save their seat" with a purse, jacket, or another item while they go through a buffet, causing some confusion.

Kids seating at the Mitzvah is acceptable at rounds and given place cards, with long rectangle tables, on furniture or in the "kids section." If kids are not assigned, consider still having a kid's sign near the place cards so they don't look for their place card. Otherwise parents looking for their kid's card or kids may question their invitation and feel less welcome

SECTION 14: SCHEDULING

Follow a schedule to ensure your event goes as planned. At least two days before your event be sure to send a copy of the schedule to your contact for your:

- band or DJ
- banquet captain or catering director
- decorator or décor company
- florist
- friends and/or family helpers
- lighting company
- miscellaneous entertainment - casino tables, magician, etc.
- photographer
- rental companies – backdrop, chairs, pipe and drape, tables, etc.)
- security guard(s)
- venue
- videographer

> **TIP:** more details ensure that everyone knows exactly what they are supposed to do and when they are supposed to do it.

Sample long and short skeleton schedules follow, so adjust your time-line according to your ceremony, for example, morning and havdalah schedules.

The long schedule acts as your planner; the short schedule is for all vendors. As you finalize things take away the blank lines and continue to update throughout the planning process. Breathe and have fun!

Mitzvah Long Schedule
For _____
Hosts _____

DAY:	DATE:

Event Company: SAVE The DATE, LLC events and promotions your way
Licensed and Insured

Event Planner Contact: Phone: Cell: Email:
Day of Director Contact: Phone: Cell: Email:
Service location: Contact: Phone: Cell: Email:
Address:
Party location: **Contact:**   **Phone:**   **Cell:**   **Email:**
Address:

Updates to schedule/date and initial here: _____
Hosts' Drinks of Choice: _____

Vendor Notes: VERY IMPORTANT TO READ OVER _____
Vendor attire_____ Band/DJ _____, vendor load in area _____, vendor meals _____, Parking _____
No Tip Jars, Please SAVE convenient parking for guests, Trash Cans/vendor items (boxes/bags) hidden from attendee's sightlines
Theme: _____

Your Notes Here: _____

Important Deadlines: _____
- Search for "Save The Dates" _____
- Order "Save The Dates" _____
- Mail out "Save The Dates" _____
- Search for invitations _____
- Order Invitations _____ Order Stamps _____
- Mail invitations _____
- Order Kippot _____
- Send photo to Temple for newsletter _____
- Select Favors/welcome bags _____
- Order favors/welcome bags _____
- Montage – must arrive on a Flash Drive to DJ/MC at least 3 weeks before event _____
- SHARE THIS SCHEDULE WITH VENDORS (Caterer, DJ, etc.) 2 weeks before event _____

TBD:
- Provide venue with list of all items they need to provide
- Confirm all vendor delivery and pick-up times with vendors and adjust on schedule
- Confirm setup and breakdown time with venue
- Honoree to meet with DJ/MC and/or Band leader prior to party - BRING SCHEDULE
- Consider times of photos/events so family knows responsibilities needed for travel arrangements

THURSDAY	DATE:

TBD   final meeting with party planner
- Bring copies of contracts, layouts, et.
- changes to: BEO, schedule, table lists, speeches, and more

TUESDAY	DATE:

email all vendors copy of long schedule, short schedule, layout and logo ...

WEDNESDAY	DATE:

- TBD_ Nail appointment

THURSDAY	DATE:

- **Deliver Box A to ceremony location**/temple - see Box/Bag A Below
- **Deliver Box B to party location**   - See Box/Bag B Below
- **Deliver welcome bags to hotel** – directions and letter
- **Call** all vendors to confirm if no response from email

Let your VIPs (family, important friends, etc.) know the details of the day/weekend

- __ **Hotel guests begin arriving, Hotel Name**_____
  Contact Name: Phone: Cell: Email:

- **1:00** hair appointments/makeup **Co. Name:** _____
  Contact Name: Phone: Cell: Email:

- _____ **Rehearsal and photos** at ceremony location
  - needs: program, tallit/kippot, siddur
  -

- **2:30** **Photographer arrives Co. Name:** _____
  Contact Name: Phone: Cell: Email:

- **3:00** **Videographer arrives Co. Name:** _____
  Contact Name: Phone: Cell: Email:
  How many coming?

- _____ **linens/other arrive** at _____ if shipped **Co. Name:** _____
  Contact Name: Phone: Cell: Email:
  Confirm arrival: _____

FRIDAY	**DATE:**

- **2:00** **Rental company arrives/linens arrive Co. Name:** _____
  Contact Name: _____ Phone: _____ Cell: _____ Email: _____
  items:

- **2:00** **Florist arrives Co. Name:** _____
  Contact Name: _____ Phone: _____ Cell: _____ Email: _____
  delivers floral arrangements to the temple

- **2:30** consider hospitality room in guest hotel

- **6:30** temple services begin
  needs: kippot, siddur, tallit

- **8:00** Shabbat dinner – out-of-towner's dinner/dessert/hospitality room
  needs:
  décor:

SATURDAY	DATE:

Ceremony location_____
Box/Bag A
    kippot _____, basket _____, Invitation _____, programs _____, Kiddush items _____,
    Yaad ____, speeches ____
(above items should get cut and pasted below next to the appropriate person providing the item)

- Planner provides_____
- Client provides_____
- Temple provides _____

    - Items above to be set up by _____ at ceremony location

- **9:00_ Family arrives at temple/ceremony** _____
  Photos may happen here

- **9:30_ Services at temple/ceremony** _____
  needs:
  coat room

- **10:30_ caterer arrives for Kiddush Co. Name:** _____
  Contact Name: Phone: Cell: Email:
  needs:

- **12:00_ kiddush or extended kiddush** _____
  Needs:
  decor:

- **2:00_ Hair appointment Co. Name:** _____
  Contact Name: Phone: Cell: Email:
  Needs:

- **TBD_ Transportation Co. Name:** _____
  Contact Name: Phone: Cell: Email:
  Needs:
  Bus adult(s): _____   Cell: _____

Venue/Party Location_____

- **Set up can begin at:** _____
    - (Generally, venues allow 2 hours before - this is important to manipulate depending on your set-up requirements 2 hours is always needed/sometimes more is needed but may not be allowed or known until you decide on your decor)

SAVE The DATE will arrive 2 hours before event start time as per contract unless previously arranged.
(note - If vendors complete their obligations and leave prior to our contracted arrival time it may affect your planner's ability to answer and address questions and issues - when needed)

Vendor arrival times - please note: This is imperative to your schedule for several reasons:
Loading dock capability
Room photos to accurately take place appx 20 min before doors open
Event Day of Planner to be available for sign/off, questions, issues - when needed
Early guests arrival time

- **4:30_ ☐ Caterer arrives Co. Name:** _____
  Contact Name: Phone: Cell: Email:
  Number of Staff: ___
  details/needs:

- **5:00_ ☐ Day of planner arrives: Co. Name:** _____
  Contact Name: Phone: Cell: Email:
  Number of Staff: ___
  details/needs:

- **5:15_ ☐ Lighting company arrives Co. Name:** _____
  Contact Name: Phone: Cell: Email:
  Number of Staff: ___
  details/needs:

- **5:20_ ☐ Decorator arrives Co. Name:** _____
  Contact Name: Phone: Cell: Email:
  Number of Staff: ___
  details/needs:

- **5:25_** ☐ **Cake/Desserts arrives Co. Name:** _____
  Contact Name: Phone: Cell: Email:
  Number of Staff: ___
  details/needs:

- **5:25_** ☐ **DJ/band arrives Co. Name:** _____
  Contact Name: Phone: Cell: Email:
  Number of Staff: ___
  details/needs:

- **5:45_** ☐ **Other entertainment arrives Co. Name:** _____
  Contact Name: Phone: Cell: Email:
  Number of Staff: ___
  details/needs:

- **6:15_** ☐ **Photographer arrives Co. Name:** _____
  Contact Name: Phone: Cell: Email:
  Number of Staff: ___
  details/needs:

- **6:30_ Senior Director to finish set-up and focus solely on party**

- **6:30_** ☐ **Videographer arrives Co. Name:** _____
  Contact Name: Phone: Cell: Email:
  Number of Staff: ___
  details/needs:

- **6:40_ room is completely ready for room photos**

- **6:40_** ☐ **Valet arrives Co. Name:** _____
  Contact Name: Phone: Cell: Email:
  Number of Staff: ___
  details/needs:

- **6:45_** ☐ **security arrives Co. Name:** _____
  Contact Name: Phone: Cell: Email:
  Number of Staff: ___
  details/needs:

- **6:45_ Guests begin arriving**
  coat room:
  family changes into party outfits

- **7:00_   COCKTAIL HOUR**

Box/Bag B
Sign in item ___, pens ___, candle lighting items ___, favors, entertainment_____, montage___,
place cards_____, teen seating sign_____, miscellaneous decorations_____,
challah____, wine glass_____, envelope box_____, logo_____, cocktail napkins_____, bathroom napkins_____, bathroom accessories_____, bags, socks_____, sock basket____, ear plugs_____ , linen ____, linen napkins ____, decor _____etc.
(above items should get cut and pasted below next to the appropriate person providing the item)

- Venue provides_____
- Planner provides_____
- Client provides_____

  - items to be set up by _____at party location

Adults go to:

Room:

Menu:
Bar:
Entertainment:

Kids – go to:

Room:

Menu:
Bar:
Entertainment:
Presentations by friends, unless later (with videographer or someone to tape it)

- **8:00_ RECEPTION**

Room:

Cocktail/entertainment ends; main room opens with dancing music
Close bars and entertainment for a short time
décor:
Linens:

- 8:10_ introductions of _____; continue dancing
- 8:17_ welcome speech by _____

- 8:20_ challah by: _____   wine by: _____
  - needs: challah, wine, Kiddush cup, challah cover, kippot
- 8:25_ adult salad is served; kids buffet opens
- 8:40_ teen games/background music/presentations/group photo
- 8:45_ main course served to adults
- 9:10_ Candle lighting – all kids sit on dance floor
  - needs: candle lighting items, linen napkin, plate, speech, music
- 9:25_ hora and dance set – lift who _____
  - needs: chair with arms
- 9:45_ _____ setup exit favors - alphabetical order/tagged
- 10:40_ dessert
- 10:50_ montage played by _____
  - needs: montage, equipment
- 11:00_ father/daughter dance or mother/son dance – all join in song: ____
  - dancing continues for the rest of the party
- 11:10_ full Circle dance - kick it up until the end
- 11:15_ kids get favors now or as they leave – take photos of favors
- 11:30_ the end

Security ensure that kids do not leave the party without parent(s) - stays 15-30 min after

- 11:30_ decorator/lighting company/other return to break down
- 12:30_ all vendors must be out

Collect all leftover favors, flowers, food/cake, and printed items; kippot; sign-in
Consider copying lists from above here as well
Centerpieces _____ (number) to be distributed to _____
Who will assist with transporting items to pack up? _____
If things are staying overnight - can they? _____

SUNDAY	DATE:

- _____returns for pick ups
- 10- 12_ Brunch_____
  - needs:

MONDAY	DATE:

- 10:00_ Rental company returns to pick up rental items

Mitzvah Short Schedule
For _____
Hosts _____

DAY:	DATE:

Event Company: SAVE The DATE, LLC events and promotions your way
Licensed and Insured

Event Planner Contact: Phone: Cell: Email:
Day of Director Contact: Phone: Cell: Email:
Service location: Contact: Phone: Cell: Email:
Address:

Party location: **Contact:**   **Phone:**   **Cell:**   **Email:**
Address:

Updates to schedule/date and initial here: _____
Hosts' Drinks of Choice: _____

Vendor Notes: VERY IMPORTANT TO READ OVER _____
Vendor attire_____ Band/DJ ____, vendor load in area ___, vendor meals ___, Parking _____
No Tip Jars, Please SAVE convenient parking for guests, Trash Cans/vendor items (boxes/bags) hidden from attendee's sightlines
     Theme: _____

9:30	**Service Location** • services begin • vendor X, Y, and Z arrive
5:00	**Party Location** • set-up can begin • vendor X, Y, and Z arrive
6:30 6:40	• clients arrive • room ready for room shots
7:00	• cocktail hour • adults to _____ • kids to _____ • presentations in kid's room
8:00	• dinner/Dancing reception

© SAVE *The* DATE, LLC EVENTS
events and promotions your way
WWW.SaveTheDateLLCEvents.com

	•	close bars and entertainment temporarily
8:10	• •	introduction of _____ continue dancing
8:17	•	all sit welcome speech by _____
8:20	• •	challah by:____ wine by: _____
8:25	• •	adult salad served kids buffet opens
8:40	•	teen games/background music/presentations/group photo
8:45	•	main course served to adults
9:10	•	candle lighting – all kids sit on dance floor
9:25	• •	hora and dance set – lift who dancing continues
9:45	•	_____ setup exit favors - alphabetical order/tagged
10:40	•	Dessert
10:50	•	montage – kids sit on dance floor
11:00 11:10	• • • •	father/daughter dance or mother/son dance – all join in song _____ dancing continues Full Circle Dance
11:15	•	favors outside or as kids leave
11:30 12:30	• • •	party is over vendors return for pick up Breakdown concludes

Day of the Event

Suggestions for the day of your event ...

- Try to eat ahead of time. You and/or the honoree may not have a chance to eat much or may not be hungry with all the excitement.

- Consider bringing flip flops, socks, or some other comfortable footwear in case your shoes become intolerable during the long day.

- Pack a few extra important items and extra clothing, just in case -- aspirin, eye drops, safety pins, socks, a tie, tissues, etc.

- Provide anyone who will be assisting with set-up with a list or diagram specifying where tables, food stations, bars, band or DJ equipment, etc. go.

- Leaving a suggested #Hashtag on the tables so guests have a way to tag every photo and video from your event on is a great way to get as much digital media as possible during the event in case the photographer or videographer misses something.

- Look around your room(s) at the reception before the event starts to make sure everything is as you expect it to be. Check for specific details.

- Have a quick meeting or "pep talk" with your vendors before the event to review your schedule of events so they understand your expectations.

- Spend a few quality minutes with each of your guests, especially, *aunts, uncles, grandparents, family friends, and those who have traveled a long way to be with you.*

Items To Deliver Or To Bring Along

It may be helpful to organize important items into boxes designated for the ceremony and the reception. Some things you might to remember include:

Box 1(A) – Ceremony Items:
- décor for ceremony and kiddush lunch
- extra invitation(s) for display in-front of kippot
- extra program(s)
- kippot basket and invitation for display
- kiddush cup
- kippot and clips
- linen for kippot/program table
- speech notes
- tallit for honoree and father/brothers

Box 2(B) – Reception Items:
- basket for socks
- bathroom décor and primping items
- bathroom guest towels
- band giveaways
- benchers
- candles (15), candelabra, and matches/lighter (for the candle lighting)
- centerpieces
- challah, challah cover, knife, and kiddush Cup
- cocktail napkins
- copies of contracts, schedules, etc.
- earplugs
- emergency items (*safety pins, scissors, Advil, etc.*)
- favors (in alphabetical order by last name)
- havdalah set
- kosher wine and kippot(s) (*for the blessing*)
- layout
- miscellaneous decorative items
- montage

- place cards (*in alphabetical order by last name*)
- prizes
- sign-in book/board/item and pens
- signs (kids place card sign, bus sign, etc) socks for guests
- sock basket
- speech notes
- video equipment/montage

Director Name:
Assistant Name:
Time finished checklist:

Date:

Mitzvah Event Checklist

INITIAL	TIME:	**UPON ARRIVAL:**
		• Check-in/text with Cara • Check-in and introduce yourself to the venue staff – give business cards/marketing gift

		• Remove any pamphlets or brochures from visible sight.
		• Locate Client Boxes and begin set-up….
		   ○ Place card table with place cards
		      ■ Save the clients' place card(s) for memories!
		   ○ Sign-in item with markers/pens
		• Set up bathroom items Bathroom items.

		• Cocktail Hour should be set-up First!!!!!!!! (Cocktail Napkins given to caterer for passing Hors d'oeuvres & available on bars)
		• Begin putting out A/B list.
		• Centerpieces/decorations Table numbers, menu cards or signage if applicable
		• Set-up Gift table; it should remain in a "safe" place at all times
		• Put socks in the sock basket & place on DJ/Band riser. Notify DJ/Band. • Provide DJ/Band with speeches & schedule.
		• Let security know who you are, that you are there to help them, and what you expect. Give them your cell so they can call if they need a break/to leave their spot.
		• Double check with DJ to make sure montage is ready to play. Confirm it is on Flash Drive/Digital File rather than a DVD. Test the montage.
		• Make sure tables and chairs are far enough away from dance floor for dancing; staff can walk in tight areas if necessary.
		• If Guests/Hosts are arriving early – make sure to offer them beverages or have the venue/caterer provide it

© SAVE *The* DATE, LLC EVENTS
events and promotions your way
WWW.SaveTheDateLLCEvents.com

INITIAL	TIME:	**45 MINUTES BEFORE PARTY BEGINS:**
		• Check table layout against guest list to confirm the number of chairs at specific tables!

		• Make sure Bar for adults/kid's bar are both set, ready to go, and that nothing is missing!
		    ○ (ie. Cocktail Napkins, special drink signage/décor)
		    ○ REMINDER: Certain parties should not serve from bottles; serve in glasses!
		    ○ REMINDER: Remove any tip boxes or jars from bar.

		• Try to have an all-vendor meeting before the party. ○ Make sure vendors know that they will be served food & beverages in a designated spot at a designated time; they should not eat off the guests' buffet and they should never "drink."
		• Make sure client's cocktail napkins, if applicable, are available on the adult bar /kid's bar and that caterer has cocktail napkins for passing hors d'oeuvres!
		• Check for safety hazards. • All vendor "stuff" must be hidden or locked away. ○ Remove brown "boxes"! Make sure DJ/band has unwrapped giveaways & they are ready to go!
		• Make sure the table is set for the blessing (challah, cover, filled kiddush cup/glass, knife, plate, etc.).
		• Light Candles – final decoration items done • Save The Date to take photos of the room/décor.
		• Confirm the photographer & the videographers have taken still photos before opening the door.
		• Dim the lighting for atmosphere (ballroom & cocktail hour) and allow the host(s) or family to view before opening the door for other guests. • Make sure the catering staff is ready before opening the door. • Make sure the music is ready and playing before opening the door.

		• ****As guests enter ballroom from cocktail hour, be at door with layout and table assignments to assist****
INITIAL	**TIME:**	**DURING THE PARTY:** • Taste the food to be sure it is not cold. • Check to see that tables/room are being cleared and kept clean/neat.
		• If there is no videographer, have dancer film presentations/speeches/other important moments. • Once cocktail hour ends breakdown and gather cocktail hour décor into a safe location. If appropriate to break down.
		• Make sure the caterer and the music are on the same page and work together on timing - if one makes a change the others need to be informed.
		• Check for safety hazards like broken glass on the dance floors throughout the event. **Time: _____ Time: _____ Time: _____** • Make sure the floor remains dry. **Time: _____ Time: _____ Time: _____** • Check that the bathrooms are clean during party. Replace guest towels as needed. **Time: _____ Time: _____ Time: _____**
		• Move the gift table to a safe place • Continue checking tables during the party to make sure guests are doing well – especially the hosts' table! • If there is candle lighting, check the candelabra, lighter, hosts' script and plate for candle drippings. • Make sure hosts eat and drink. • Make sure family gets photo entertainment done of themselves. • Gather items appropriate for mementos for family to take home (ie. Photo booth photos, extra place cards, stickers, signs, cocktail napkins)
		• If kids get out of hand be prepared to control the situation. o Ask security to assist & inform client if appropriate.
		• As party begins to end ask bartenders to throw some bottled water on ice to give to client(s) at end of

		party! Have extra bottles on top of bar for guests as they leave. •
INITIAL	**TIME:**	**AS GUESTS LEAVE/AT END OF PARTY:** • Get keys from hosts so their car(s) or hotel rooms are packed without delay. o DO NOT DRIVE HOSTS CAR!!!!!!!

		• Collect Items: (Refer to Box A/B List on schedule as a reminder) **Highlight each item**
		    o Centerpieces
		    o Gifts /Envelopes!
		    o Sign in items
		    o Extra cocktail napkins
		    o Bathroom accessories/Bathroom towels
		    o Food and/or alcohol TO GO (CATERER to Handle)
		• ****Give bag of envelopes received for Bar/Bat Mitzvah child in STD shopping bag!***

		• Replace any venue pamphlets that were removed in the exact location as originally set up. • Store rental linen in a trash bag in kitchen for pick up with a piece of paper indicating rental company & name of party. (ie. "Choice Party Rentals – Goldberg Bat Mitzvah") • Count linens and have 2 people sign off on numbers and take a photo.
		• Confirm with venue staff your departure or any rental/STD items to be left or stored overnight, where and when they will be picked up. (if applicable) Take a photo • Check out with Cara

SECTION 15: GUESTS

Moderate dress, usually business formal with shoulders covered, is typical for the service. Party attire is acceptable with covered shoulders.

The host has more flexibility for the party:

- black tie – men wear a tuxedo; women wear a ball or dressy gown
- black tie preferred – men wear a tuxedo or dark suit; women wear a ball gown and may substitute a dressy, dresses
- casual - dress nicely for a party, nice jeans or pants are acceptable
- creative black tie – men wear a tuxedos or black suit with something fun added; women wear dressy funky fun clothes
- funky formal – dress formally but have fun doing so
- semi-casual - wear slacks, blazers, pants, dresses or dress pants.
- semi-formal - wear suits and dresses
- tie preferred – wear suits or dresses

Sample attire wording would be:

- black tie and long gown/creative black tie
- black tie optional/Semi-formal
- basketball or casual attire
- business casual
- casual island chic
- city chic
- dress deluxe, no tux
- dress for success
- dress to impress
- evening attire
- evening cocktail attire
- funky formal
- high up commissioners
- jeans and jewels
- resort casual
- snappy casual
- exercise clothes
- party chic
- posh club attire
- tie preferred

Attire Information Sheet

Basic Information

    Company:

    Contact person:

    Phone:

    E-mail:

    Cell:

    Fax:

    Address:

Contract and Payment

    Total hours:

    Total contract:

    Contract signed:

    Total charges:

    Deposit amount:

        Due:

        Payment: Credit card

                          Check (check #:   )

    Final Payment amount:

        Due:

        Payment: Credit card

                          Check (check #:   )

Your Guests

Your guest list will affect your final budget, so decide early who is allowed to add guests (grandma and grandpa table(s), business clients, new schoolmates) and your cut-off dates. For example, your child's friends will change from 6th to the 7th grade, so carefully consider who gets a "Save the Date" card.

You want to reach that careful balance between inviting everyone you like and not breaking the budget ... is party décor or a fancier guest menu more important to you? The more guests, the less you spend per person on décor, music, photos, video and the other fixed costs. Some things cost more with each guest added. Then adult beverages cost more; children's meals cost less.

Different guests will react differently. Some RSVP's come immediately; some may never come. You will probably need to call some guests to meet your guarantee deadlines; don't assume no rsvp means a guest will not show. Some families may assume the entire family is invited, so be honest and call your guest when they rsvp an uninvited family member, or "blame it on your party planner."

Last minute cancelations for sickness or sports teams come up, so guarantee about 2-5% under your final count. Caterers almost always make 5% over the guarantee, so let them charge you later if they choose to count covers.

Likewise, guests seem to think they can take the centerpieces, so place a note by each one about not taking them -- that they are being donated or going to Aunt June. Put someone in charge of politely letting a guest know if the centerpieces are rented and "walking."

Some guests skip services, some leave early, some may dress poorly -- don't let it ruin your fun, it's not worth the anger.

Gifts
- Some guests will not bring a gift to the event, so wait a few weeks for the mail.
- Some guests will not bring any gift – as surprising as it sounds.
- Kids who are not very close friends will generally give chai or double chai ($18, $26 or keep multiplying).
- Kids could leave an envelope filled with a check <u>anywhere</u>. Have a locked decorative gift box set on a gift table before your first guest arrives.

Seating

Modern informality allows for choices - individual tables, a "U" shape, rows of tables, and others. You may have high-top tables, cocktail tables, round tables, rectangular tables, etc.

- A high-top table generally does not have chairs or stools
- A cocktail table will seat 2-6 guests
- A 5-foot round table will seat 8-10 guests depending on the size of the chair
- A 6-foot round table will seat 10-12 guests depending on the size of your chair, so use larger tables if you are tight on room so you can cut out a table

Plan seating for at least half of your guests when serving a full meal at stations and you want an active event. It isn't necessary to plan seating for the total number of guest if they will be dancing, playing games, etc. during mealtime.

- If your guests will be primarily kids, consider a room, area or section for adults
- Reserve seating for the elderly or guests with special needs

Create a diagram or layout of the room and table arrangements including table numbers or the guests and the number of people at each table. Consider:

- Seating guests with people they already know or with people you think they will get along with
    - Avoid seating guests that do not get along at the same table or nearby
    - Seat older guests away from the speakers

> TIP: Make sure your planner, caterer and other helpers have an alphabetical list of guests' names and seating assignments

Layout

A "layout" is a diagram that displays how the room will be set-up for your event.

Layouts can include

- Bar(s)
- Candle lighting table
- Cocktail hour (separate layout)
- DJ and dance floor
- Food Stations/Buffet (kids or adults)
- Gift table
- Kids area (furniture vs. tables)
- Mitzvah project and donation collection table
- Motzi table
- Place card table
- Photo booth and other entertainment
- Tables with number of chairs at each table
- Table names/numbers
- And so much more

Your venue may help you with creating a custom layout or they may provide a selection of room design layouts they have previously made that include dimensions. They may also provide a blank layout for you to draw on.

If they do not, there are many sites that can assist you with creating your layout.

Layout Samples

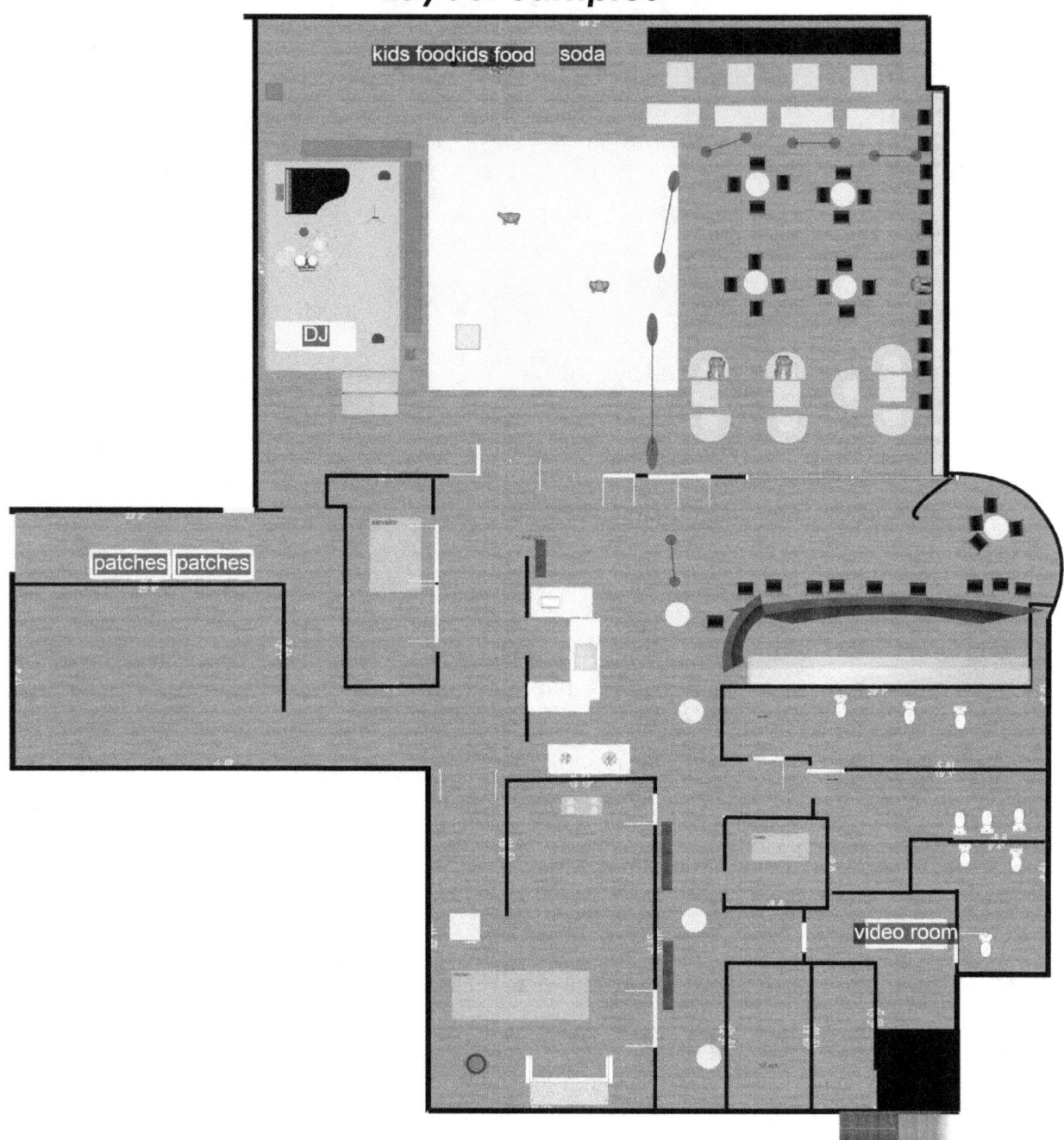

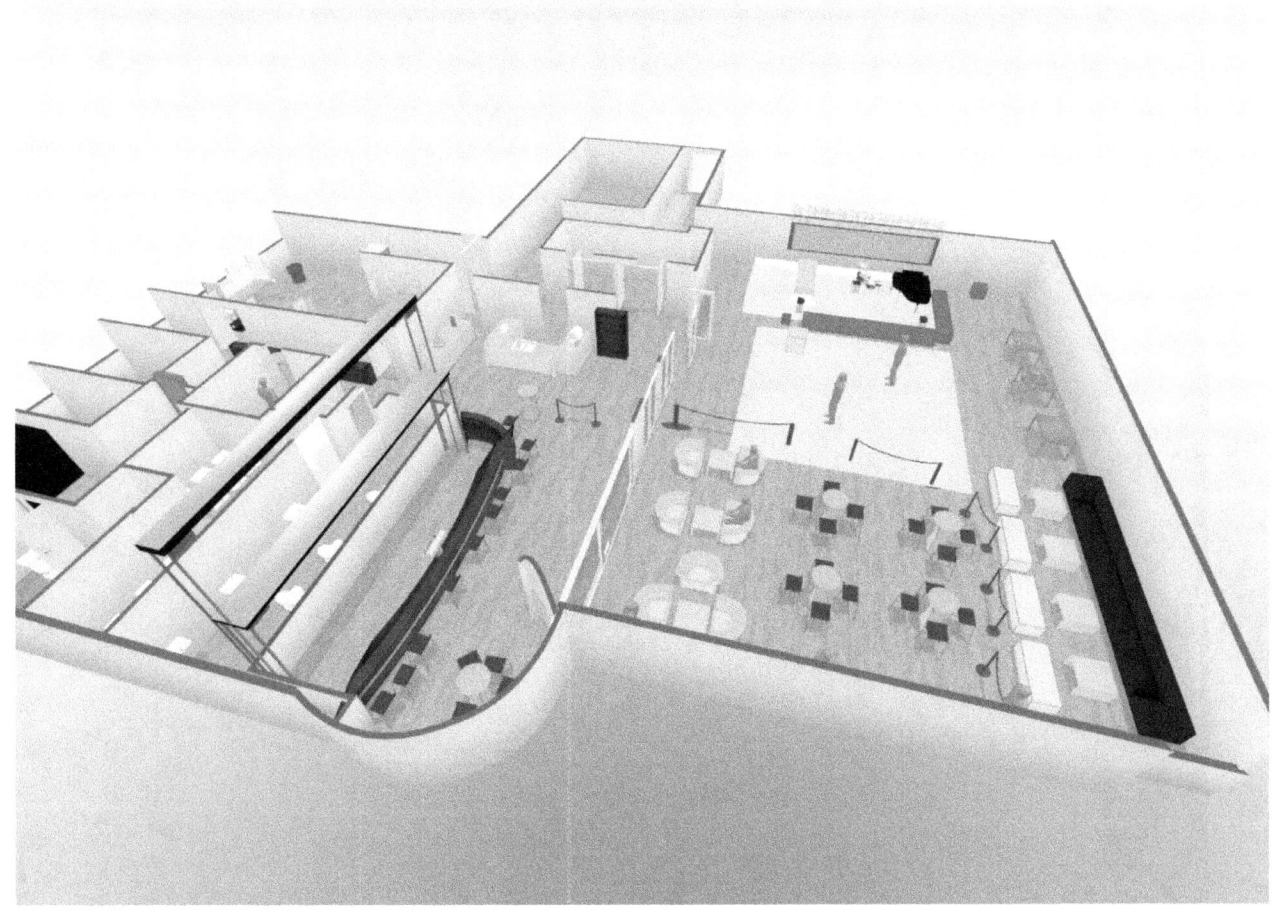

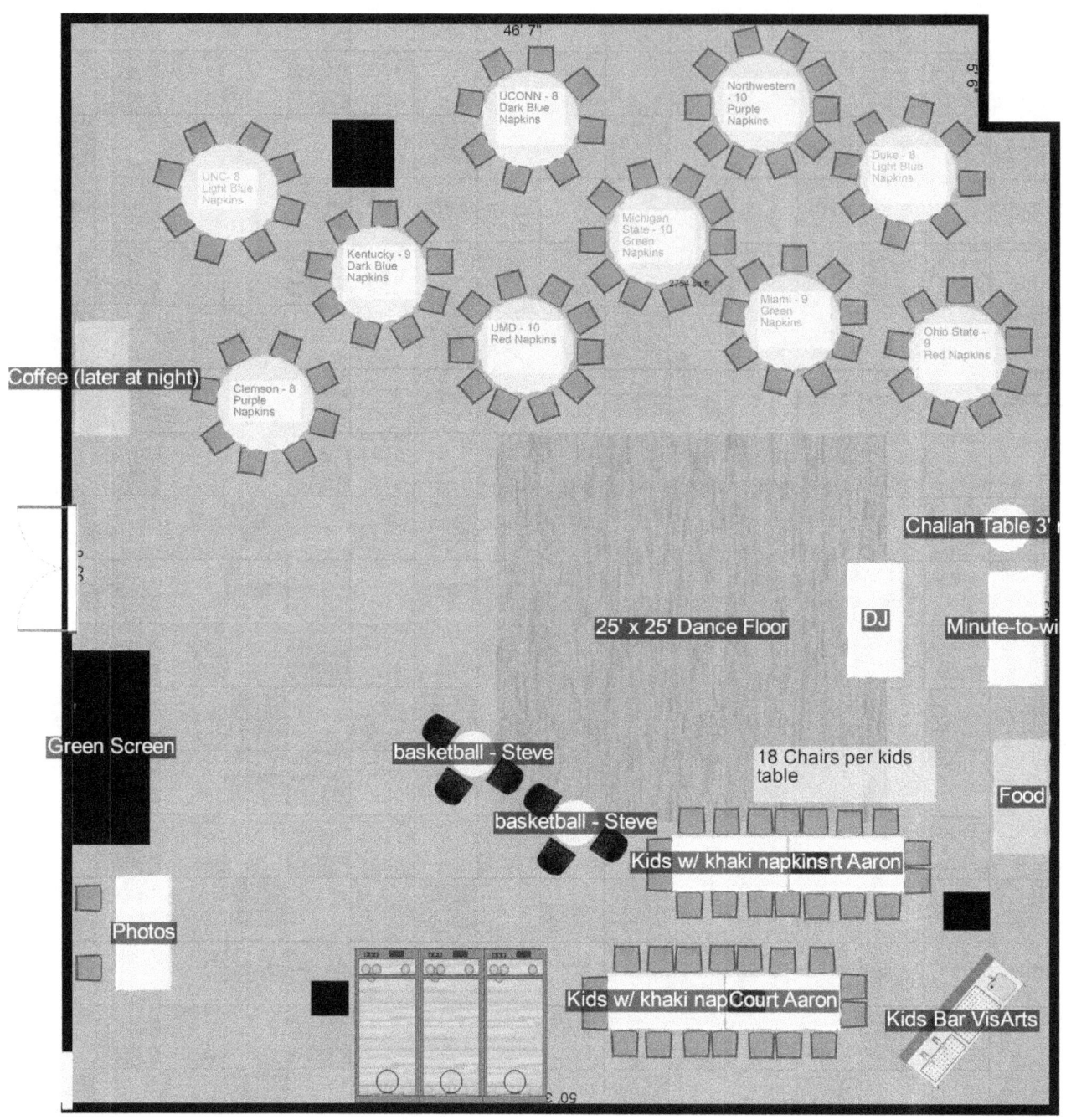

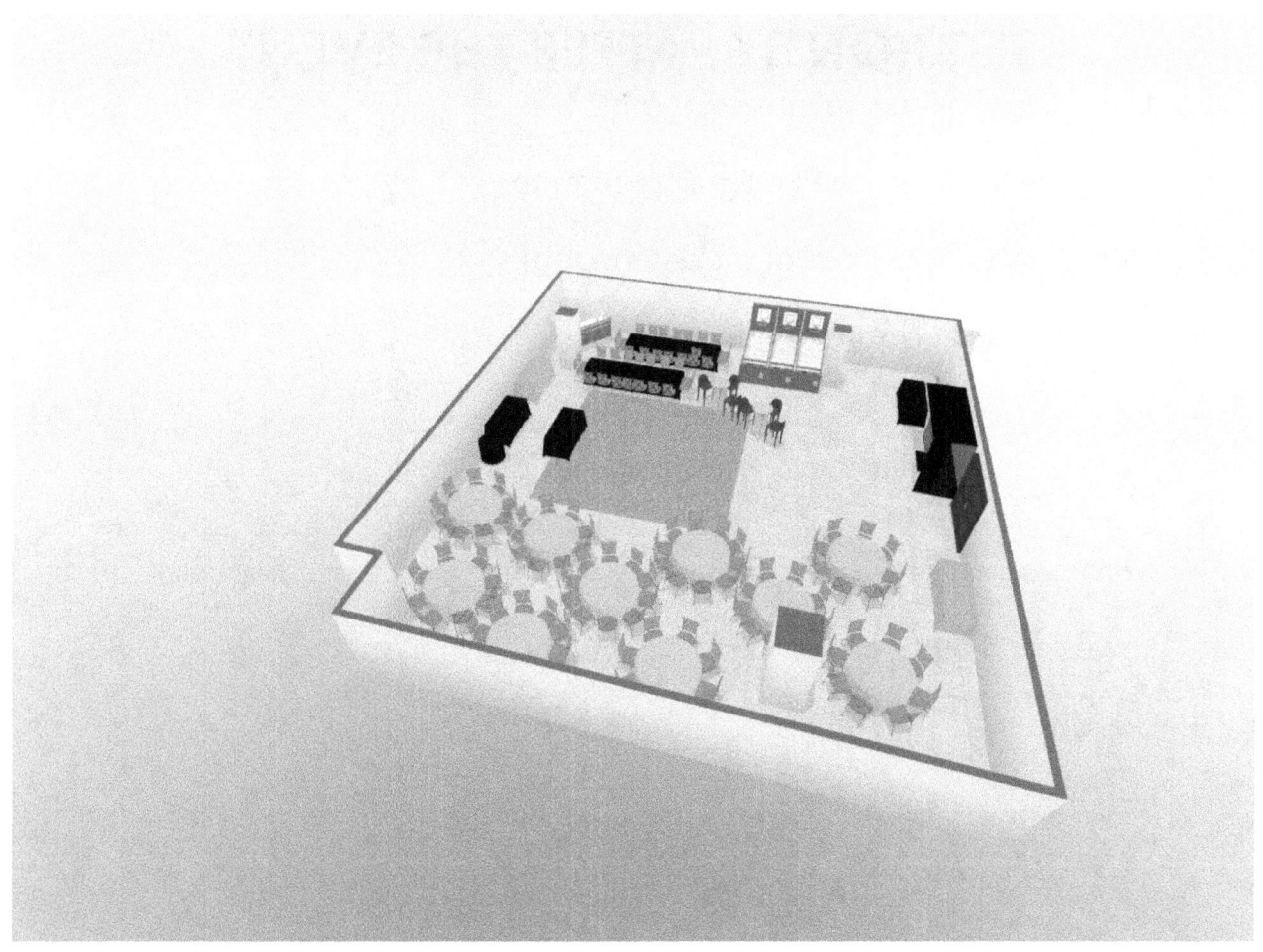

SECTION 16: AFTER THE EVENT

Collect your keepsakes, you earned them!

- a candle from the candle lighting ceremony
- a centerpiece (or parts of a centerpiece)
- extra cocktail napkins or guest towels
- extra favors
- extra invitations
- extra programs
- flowers and other decorations
- kippahs
- the challah knife
- the wine glass
- the sign-in book
- your place card

Be sure to collect your gifts and envelopes and any leftover cake, food and beverages. Do your centerpieces stay for the next brunch or get donated somewhere they need to be delivered?

Write your thank you notes.

- Print out labels with addresses or prepare the envelopes ahead of time.

- The best way to do this is to have your son or daughter write 5-10 a night until you are all finished.

Time to share your pictures and build your album

- Proofs come from your photographer about 1-2 weeks after your event either in low resolution digital format or actual photographs that you can touch and hold.

- Give yourself a time - line to get this done.

- Start by organizing your proofs and picking your favorites. Organize them in an order you would like to see them. Your photographer will then edit these photos and design your virtual album which can take up to 6 months.

- The album production then can also take up to 6 months to once you approve your proofed virtual album.

- Share low resolution photos. Use high resolution photos for printing or uploading for printing purposes.

Get your video

- Pick songs you would like on your video.

- Allow up to 2 months for video production to be finalized.

- Some videographers will get you a 3 min. highlight quickly to share on social media.

Send Thank you notes

- Vendors always appreciate your personal thank you, this is especially important if you hope to hire them again in the future.

- The Rabbi or Cantor may deserve a shout out in the Temple newsletter with a donation to their discretionary fund following your event.

Sign your child up for Confirmation classes

Next-Day Brunch Information Sheet

Basic Information

    Company:

    Contact person:

    Phone:

    E-mail:

    Cell:

    Fax:

    Address:

Information
    Decorations:
    Entertainment:
    Menu:
    Music:
    Linens:

Contract and Payment

    Total contract:

    Contract signed:

    Total charges:

    Deposit Amount:

        Due:

        Payment: Credit card

                          Check (check #:   )

    Final Payment Amount:

        Due:

        Payment: Credit card

                          Check (check #:   )

Miscellaneous Expenses Information Sheet

Basic Information

    Company:

    Contact person:

    Phone:

    E-mail:

    Cell:

    Fax:

    Address:

Information
    Total:

    Total:

Contract and Payment

    Total hours:

    Total contract:

    Contract signed:

    Total charges:

    Deposit Amount:

        Due:

        Payment: Credit card

                        Check (check #:   )

    Final Payment Amount:

        Due:

        Payment: Credit card

                        Check (check #:   )

www.ingramcontent.com/pod-product-compliance
Lightning Source LLC
Chambersburg PA
CBHW080552230426
43663CB00015B/2807